FINDING
THE DIVINE
IN EVERYDAY
PLACES

Glory
Happening

Kaitlin B. Curtice

PARACLETE PRESS
BREWSTER, MASSACHUSETTS

2017 First Printing

Glory Happening: Finding the Divine in Everyday Places

Copyright © 2017 by Kaitlin B. Curtice

ISBN 978-1-61261-896-8

The Paraclete Press name and logo (dove on cross) are trademarks of Paraclete Press, Inc.

Library of Congress Cataloging-in-Publication Data

Names: Curtice, Kaitlin B., author.
Title: Glory happening : finding the divine in everyday places / Kaitlin B.
  Curtice.
Description: Brewster, Massachusetts : Paraclete Press Inc., 2017. | Series:
  Routledge studies in ethics and moral theory ; 40
Identifiers: LCCN 2017028003 | ISBN 9781612618968 (trade paper)
Subjects: LCSH: Meditations. | Glory of God--Christianity--Meditations. |
  Kingdom of God--Meditations.
Classification: LCC BV4811 .C86 2017 | DDC 242--dc23
LC record available at https://lccn.loc.gov/2017028003

10 9 8 7 6 5 4 3 2 1

Published by Paraclete Press
Brewster, Massachusetts
www.paracletepress.com

Printed in the United States of America

To Travis, the man who is my constant;
to Eliot and Isaiah,
the boys who ask me to tell stories
and who give me stories to tell;
and to that two-bedroom apartment
where these stories were born—
I have met glory in each of you.

To live is to be slowly born.

--Antoine de Saint-Exupery

CONTENTS

INTRODUCTION

Glory: n. magnificence, great beauty.

I stand washing my dishes at the kitchen sink and look out across the apartment. My boys are wrestling on the floor, my husband works on an ever-forming PhD, and I take it all in.

Glory.

"Our life is a faint tracing on the surface of mystery, like the idle curved tunnels of leaf miners on the face of a leaf," Annie Dillard once said. "We must somehow take a wider view, look at the whole landscape, really see it, and describe what's going on here."[1]

When I stand there doing the dishes, scrubbing the cream-white countertop surfaces clean, I'm asking for something holy to happen.

If I stand there long enough, if I wait and listen and breathe, I can take it all in, and it is a sacred kind of heaviness, a glorious light, a tender prompt to worship and receive Kingdom. I recall why exactly I get to stand on holy ground and call myself blessed in a tiny space with a busy schedule and two toddlers running around me day and night.

Annie Dillard found it in a leaf, and I find it within the tiny, painted-white walls of our two-bedroom apartment.

Glory.

It is the essence of God, the kind gift of Spirit in Jesus.

Glory comes to us; glory shelters and holds us. Glory brings beauty to us, calls beauty out of us, says that we are good, in everything that we are today, and in everything that we'll be tomorrow.

Glory.

I imagine the timeline of my life. I imagine the seasons, the way they pass by on that line in the blink of an eye, the scribble of a pencil in an unsteady hand.

I think of quiet moments when I'm alone with my soul's echo and my breath's loudness, memories zooming in and out and back in again through the lens of my heart.

I watch the line grow with every experience, and then step further back, out of myself. Above and around and beyond, there's another view of that line, and its span looks vastly different in luminous light.

Jesus stretches his hand across the heavens and creates all of life, and he sweeps his eyes across the span of our lives and sees everything and *every little thing* all at once, all in an instant and in all-knowing. All of our experiences are meant to teach us something; lessons can be gleaned from the emotion of them, from the joy and pain in them, even in the minutiae of them.

Glory can happen upon them and inhabit and mold them.

When you and I look over our timelines, it's as if we are taking a blade and carving it into the wood of a tree, just for us to remember— our own little Ebenezer to show that we've seen and known God, that we have been heard and helped, right there in the coffee shop, at the work desk, in the dining room, by the oak tree in our ungroomed backyard, at the filled kitchen sink, our own promise forever claimed by the reality of a graceful and present Mystery.

In that space, our timelines become stories, and our stories become glory-truth for each other, in our deepest hurts and in our most joyous celebrations, because glory is about paying attention in every space and season—*glory* is about magnificence.

Meals are shared in comfort because we comfort each other. Secrets are given in trust because we believe in the power of company and community. And every season teaches us something, envelops us in a process of living, because I see my story and yours, and because they are varied—they are life to each of us in the most remarkable ways.

Your life and your stories show me something; my heart can show you something, too.

It's like Christmas over and over and over again, this opening up of something precious, celebrations abounding.

This is a book of stories and prayers, of everyday experiences in everyday spaces. What we choose to see is holy ground for our feet, solace for our tired and often-wandering souls, no matter how *everyday*. We choose to stop and take in *glory*; we choose a different reality.

These are prayers that I've written for my own soul. They are prayers that I pray in the quiet, words I cry out when the chaos is overwhelming to me.

They are my hopes for glory, reflections that keep me tethered to the Mystery embedded in humanity and in creation. We walk in the benevolence of community, of a life together. We all long for holy spaces, *magnificent moments,* that bring us peace.

We all long to hold more Mystery and know what we are made for. Our experiences stretch into realms that we don't understand but desperately need. May we look deeper, invest in more presence, and embrace the quiet of our souls.

I mention *Kingdom* here—a lot of talk about the Kingdom here and coming, the Kingdom almost but not yet. The Kingdom, in this case, is the daily manifestation of shalom. The Kingdom is presence, a full alertness of living here and now. It is living within the reality of peace in every circumstance. And we move toward Kingdom as we live into *glory,* in all of its manifestations for us. Like a timeline, like seasons, we experience glory as a process.

In the Christian tradition, glory is manifested in various ways throughout the Bible. This book is arranged as a series of these manifestations: creation, light, weight, voice, fire, honor, worship, and Kingdom.

May we learn to see and know God in every manifestation, and may Mystery and the discovery of our own soul's voice become our dearest friends in the search.

PART ONE:
Creation

PSALM 104:24–30

O LORD, how manifold are your works!
   In wisdom you have made them all;
   the earth is full of your creatures.
Yonder is the sea, great and wide,
   creeping things innumerable are there,
   living things both small and great.
There go the ships,
   and Leviathan that you formed to sport in it.
These all look to you
   to give them their food in due season;
when you give to them, they gather it up;
   when you open your hand, they are filled with good things.
When you hide your face, they are dismayed;
   when you take away their breath, they die
   and return to their dust.
When you send forth your spirit, they are created;
   and you renew the face of the ground.

1. THE NEW WORLD

Everything looked fresh, and the new green of Spring was shimmering in the fields and on the tips of the trees' fingers. —J.R.R. TOLKIEN, *FELLOWSHIP OF THE RING*[2]

*W*hen we moved to Georgia, I went to a bustling coffee shop called Dancing Goats with a pile of books shoved into my purse. I read about being quiet, and I listened to Ben Howard as loud as I could in my little earbuds. Ben called out for more life and more adventure. He understood something I didn't, saw something ahead of me yet to be discovered.

I read from Thomas Merton and Brennan Manning, tiny pieces of the monastic life coming alive in me in ways I could not yet understand.

I took notes and underlined full pages; I listened and felt the muscles of my soul being stretched into some different shape. I was being molded into someone entirely new, the very essence of transforming power taking root inside of me.

Thomas Merton once said,

> The will of the Lord is not a static center drawing our souls blindly toward itself. It is a creative power, working everywhere, giving life and being and direction to all things, and above all forming and creating, in the midst of an old creation, a whole new world which is called the Kingdom of God.[3]

Glory.

There, the door to reading and writing blew wide open, into a green space I'd never seen before, let alone imagined, even through the wildest beauty of Narnia. A world of authors I'd never heard of seemed to meet me at my doorstep—the words of Barbara Brown Taylor, Annie Dillard, Anne Lamott, Brother David Steindl-Rast,

Richard Rohr, Randy Woodley, and Erika Morrison speaking truth to all the spaces in my spirit that were shifting and trying to create something new.

I'd sit on my balcony garden later in the day, surrounded by basil towers and celosias, zinnias and spindles of rosemary, and Barbara Brown Taylor would seem to lean in and say, "People encounter God under shady oak trees, on riverbanks, at the tops of mountains, and in long stretches of barren wilderness."[4]

And I'd sit back and watch the trees swaying in the wind around my apartment complex. And I'd ask God what was happening with me there, where those little child-steps were leading me.

And I'd keep reading.

"God shows up in the whirlwinds," Barbara would whisper, "in the starry skies, burning bushes, and perfect strangers. When people want to know more about God, the son of God tells them to pay attention to the lilies of the field and the birds of the air, to women kneading bread and workers lining up for their pay."[5]

And the more I read Barbara's words, the more they became the soft-spoken words of my own heart—a response to the journey I'd started in 2014 when we moved to sunny Georgia, and the journey I began in order to learn more about my Native American heritage.

I sat and felt life beside me—those little bright beings reaching their arms up toward the sun, digging their heels into the comfort of their home soil. I could hear the seeds whisper, their quiet, soft hearts beckoned from the womb of dirt to the waiting outside air.

It's all life, all abundance.

Not just the husky at my feet, but the red ink on my page, the cream in my coffee, the towering basil.

They all speak one deep breath of *hallelujah* and *amen*.

I closed the book for a moment, closed off the new world in which I had begun to live perpetually—a world of new truth, new listening, all learning, all wide-eyed wonder. I closed the book and took a deep breath and whispered *thank you* to the life God had started creating in me.

You are the stillness in this place.
Holy One, Kingdom come.
Embrace us here, now.
Speak into our hollow places
where we've lost our words and find only
utterances, only experiences
and observations to teach us who you are.
Secure us by your kind mercy.
Jesus, speak in the quiet.
Give us rest.
Amen.

2. THE CHRISTMAS FLOOD

In the end, gratefulness will be our full aliveness to a gratuitously given world. —BROTHER DAVID STEINDL-RAST[6]

When we drive from Georgia where we currently live back to the Midwest, we go up and over, north and west, through hills and hills of green grass and low-hanging skies.

It's a beautiful drive every time, and exceedingly long.

We pass through Tennessee, Kentucky, Illinois, and on into Missouri, back through the Ozark Mountains we once called home. The flat cornfields and cow pastures bring an unexpected calm, like an open hand that says *come on in, all are welcome here.*

But last Christmas, a big flood hit the states.

We drove back south and saw the same fields we'd passed on the way in, covered with standing water.

Trees were only showing their top halves, leafless and cold.

The flood covered everything—rivers risen almost to bridges, and whole highway sections closed.

Eliot, my oldest son, was mesmerized by it; he kept saying how sad it was that everything was buried in water, how sad that we couldn't see those pretty plains we'd come to adore.

I agreed with him, but on a long stretch of open road, while everyone else in my family slept, I drove and thought about that water covering the hills around me.

A flood is a funny thing.

For all the grief that can come with it, it also brings a deep and full cleansing, wiping everything away to start again—new spaces, new grasses, spreading seeds, and digging up roots.

Maybe the trees said, "Finally, I can drink my fill; my roots have been so thirsty for so long."

And maybe the grass whispered, "In the spring I will be greener than ever, because this water has given me new life."

We humans, though, we see our basements flooded and our homes evacuated and a few people lost to the current, and say, *How can this be made of any good?*

After the boys woke up, we drove in that rain and talked about it, about how there are two sides to every coin, two separate views to see life through, and a lot of overlap in between.

And the hard and unbelievable truth is that we walk both at the same time. We hold hope and despair, one in each arm, and we cradle them close to our chest, because they both have something important to say at every moment.

And we turn to our children and try to help them understand, and we look to the left and the right at those hills buried in water and whisper as much as we can, "Kingdom come. Oh come, Kingdom."

Jesus,
You have a full view from where you stand,
and we are quite limited here.
Our eyes are biased,
our hearts attracted to every emotion possible,
and we feel each one deep,
to the core of who we are.
And you feel, too,
but you feel in a fuller way.
You feel the pulse of the earth,
you feel the pulse of us,
you feel the pulse of your
own holy heart
and the Spirit
whisper to
remain close and
be still
and give us
everything we need
to get through
everything we endure.
You, then,
are everything to us.
Fully,
always,
everything.
Amen.

3. THE PRACTICE OF PATIENCE

The only reality I can describe with any accuracy is my own limited experience of what I think may be God: the More, the Really Real, the Luminous Web That Holds Everything in Place. —BARBARA BROWN TAYLOR[7]

*B*ecause we have a balcony garden, I use two recycled milk jugs to hydrate my plants each day. I go to the kitchen sink, put the open container under the faucet, and wait.

It takes a little while—to my severely impatient self, too long—for the jug to fill all the way. And there's not much I can do in that space except watch and tap my foot on the floor and sip my ever-cooling coffee.

But finally, one day, I realize how thankful I am for this moment, for this small act of glory. I walk the jugs out to the small balcony and slowly water all of my plants, slowly speak over them, calling them to come higher, to climb toward the sky so I can see them in all their beauty.

That water feeds mint and rosemary, a little sprig of cilantro trying to decide what she'll do in the next few days. It gives life to all those zinnias and marigolds that sprouted up from their beginning seeds. And every bit of their growth, their slow and steady rise to the sky, seems to take forever.

There aren't many ways to force ourselves into the waiting anymore, not the way our lives seem to thrust themselves along in constant busyness.

I've never ached and longed for the quiet like I do now. And I've never cherished acts of patience like I do now.

These things are hardest for me:

to sit and rest when I could be cleaning, cooking, working, moving, creating;

to stop and wait when I could be hustling about, active and frantic.

It's this little practice of patience, filling these milk cartons a few times a day, that keeps me tethered.

Sometimes I think as people—maybe especially as Millennials—we're constant drifters:

to the newest fad,
to the newest scene,
on to the next season,
into the next home.

And before we realize it, we've flown everywhere and never really landed.

But I need to be tethered.

I want to be content, quiet, resourceful, kind. And so, I absolutely need to be more patient.

And if I have to keep a Georgia garden on my balcony all year long to remind me of my need for hydration, of my need to refill that milk jug over and over again, then I will let it be my holy act, a reminder of my salvation, that when I am thirsty, someone is there to give me drink.

O God,
Call us into the good work.
And when we are unable,
push us into the sunlight,
and let us see your face.
Hydrate our souls
with the kind power of your Mystery.
There, we will understand.
There, we will not be afraid.
Because there,
the darkness is only a fraud.
Amen.

4. LESSONS FROM OUR HUSKY

My experience of being and your experience of being are exactly the same—the boundaryless, wordless, woosh of suchness. —Steven Levine[8]

When I was pregnant with each of my boys, our husky, Sam, knew.

He was more protective, more aware. He'd sit closer to me than usual, curl up at my feet, sniff my belly as if to say, *Hello in there, I've got everything under control until you arrive.*

He's been my constant protector in the eight years we've owned him.

When my husband, Travis, went to India for ten days to teach with his father, Sam slept on the bed with me. He stayed by my side, leaving evidence in a trail of thick, bristled fur from the corner of the bed across the floor in a distinct path where he walked behind me.

Dogs seem to have that extra sense about them, and I think maybe we've got something to learn from them, busied and distracted people that we are. Maybe we need to see each other better, to use senses that we've long ago forsaken to help us remember the ways in which we are connected to each other.

If Sam could read the movements happening deep inside my body when my boys were growing there, what might we be missing in the way we care for each other every single day?

Maybe if I look deeper into my husband's eyes, I can see something he's not telling me, meet a need that hasn't even been asked to be met.

If I take a moment longer to spend time with a friend, I might understand her joys and sorrows better and give a response of love, whatever the situation.

You and I, we are perpetual learners, aren't we? And people, we're perpetual changers, too.

Let's seek each other out, use our senses and respond in love, igniting sparks of *glory* anywhere they may be found.

We're moving out of our apartment and into a house soon, and my son Eliot is sure we are moving to a place of peace. He told us that the "wind of wolves howls when we get close to our house," because he's sensing something we're not.

He's understanding that life flows and bleeds beneath the surface, that things happen when we can't see them.

When we feel and know and understand with our deep parts, we enter into an unseen vein of life, and that is where needs are met. A simple home becomes a place that holds wind and breath and holiness, a space for us to know each other, to be known, and to become something better from one day to the next.

We learn it in the stoic presence of our eleven-year-old dog, who walks the wood floors with his big paws and reminds us that he sees each of us for who we are and always have been.

Jesus,
Where there is a need,
show it to me.
Look me in the eyes
through the eyes
of someone I can see,
someone I can tangibly care for
or listen to
or hold close.
Show me how to use
all of my senses
to understand
the way your Kingdom
brings all of our senses
to life.
Amen.

5. AT THE TABLE

If more of us valued food and cheer and song above hoarded gold, it would be a merrier world. —J. R. R. TOLKIEN, *THE HOBBIT*[9]

One day, Eliot and I gathered in our tiny kitchen to bake bread. He scooped the yeast into the big green bowl—one, two, three, four, five—until it covered the water and honey.

We stirred in the flour.

"What does *yeast* mean, Mommy?" Eliot asked.

"Yeast makes it really yummy and fluffy when we bake it," I said.

I could have told him more, if I understood it myself. But the truth of baking this bread is that it is just as magical to me as it is to my toddlers. I wait an hour and watch how the flour, heavy as it is, becomes consumed by little bubbles, light as a feather, overflowing the top of the green mixing bowl.

Now that he is a little bigger, Eliot makes his own bread, mixes a little yeast with flour and honey and salt and water and rolls it out on the counter. We pop it into the oven for fifteen minutes and cut it into fourths when it is just browned. It is a celebration of his newfound love for baking, for touch and sight and smell.

The table is slowly becoming a place of simplicity, of vegetables and ripening fruit, cheese and bread, of constant conversation over what kind of day we're having and negotiations over how many bites Eliot has to take before he can leave the table and go play again—where my other son Isaiah climbs up on top, trying to grab the pepper grinder and eat the grains of salt as they fall to the tablecloth from our little red star-shaped salt dishes.

And sometimes, in a moment of quiet when I see my own family huddled around me, I sit back and think of *them,* my Native American ancestors who lived so long ago in the peace of their own spaces.

I think back to my great-great-grandmothers and the crops they toiled over, the long work over pits of fire, beating out dough every single day, the food that came to their tables for their families to gather and tell stories, to rest from the work and take small, slow breaths together before digging back into their work again.

I think of how they used every bit of everything they had, using corn husks to make sleeping mats and dolls and clothing after the hominy was cultivated by those same hands.

They reached for God, too, in the callusing of their fingertips.

We watch for hours as the dough rises, as we eat meals and play games and read books. The yeast works constantly, the honey marinates, seeps into the flour's very being.

Yeast brings that dough to life, calls every fiber to the surface, billowed up and over its own edges.

Hours later, I take three loaves of honey wheat bread out of the oven and slather them with butter, and Eliot watches and Isaiah reaches for it, because it's all ours and it's all holy, that space we share in the corner of our kitchen where our souls billow up, asking for grace to rise and cover us.

Jesus,
It will take us our whole lives and all of eternity
to understand how exactly you
came to be the bread and the wine.
It will take us our whole lives and all of eternity
to understand how exactly you
offer yourself to us in such a way.
We do not fathom it,
and so we cannot fathom you.
But we will spend our whole lives and all of eternity
trying.
Amen.

6. PRAYER FLAGS

If one advances confidently in the direction of his dreams, and endeavors to live the life which he has imagined, he will meet with a success unexpected in common hours. —HENRY DAVID THOREAU[10]

*I*n the middle of a community garden in the heart of Atlanta, someone strung up a row of prayer flags across the top of their produce. I saw these pictures and symbols floating in the breeze, unfamiliar with their meaning, sure that they were something sacred to the gardener who placed them there.

A few months later, we moved into a house and had three tomato plants growing up from the ground in the front yard, a gift from our landlord. I pictured there in the bare air above them a series of colored flags, calling out to all passersby to stop and notice the awe-inspiring work of growth going on there.

After a little googling, I discovered they were Tibetan prayer flags, used outside to call good things from all corners of the earth.

Our friend Daniel was on a trip all summer and posted a picture of similar flags on a mountaintop, calling for fresh life through the breeze carrying them. And I knew that those colored pieces of cloth were supposed to be something important for me, something holy in my own space of asking and seeking and becoming new in the presence of my own Native American heritage with God.

While I was gone from the house one morning a few weeks later, our dear friend Rick came by with a gift from his recent trip to India.

I received a text message from Travis with a picture—colored flags hanging in the living room from my guitar rack—and I knew: through the kindness of a friend who does not believe as I do, God had brought something home to me.

Later that day in my living room, I carefully touched the flags, very quietly noticed the frayed edges of each. Rick got them for me at the site where Buddha received his vision, a holy site for people to come and pray and remember.

I put the flags on our front porch, because they are meant to be outside, to be a welcoming mark. They are meant to bring something good, to create peace and grace.

And when I see them, I am brought back to myself again, and back to all the voices who pray to God, and to Buddha, through the years, to those forces that call for benevolence and holiness and something sacred in the midst of a hectic life.

Jesus,
We go through life assuming that you journey with us
only at certain points, that only specific moments
    catch your eye.
But in truth, you journey with us everywhere
and through everything.
You are there in the beginning,
and you are with us through every new experience,
in every space that we inhabit,
every season that calls us to ourselves
and to the people around us.
You journey with us because your
goodness is constant,
and in that goodness we are,
of course,
never alone.
Hallelujah,
that you have always been
one who journeys.
Hallelujah,
that you do not abandon the
task.
Amen.

PART TWO:
Light

JOHN 8:12

Again Jesus spoke to them, saying, "I am the light of the world. Whoever follows me will never walk in darkness but will have the light of life."

7. SABBATH

Life without touching other people is boring as hell. —GLENNON
DOYLE MELTON[11]

*L*eanna and Aaron hosted a Shabbat dinner one Friday
night, a new investment in recognizing and practicing
Sabbath rest every week. There were eight adults and our
two boys, who came bustling through the door like it was a birthday
party for the two of them.

We hugged hello and gathered close to the kitchen, because it's
always the heart of the home. I tossed the salad, and Eliot came running in, his face beaming.

"Kwazii, Mom, it's Kwazii!" he yelled as he held up a coloring
page, his favorite cartoon character printed on a sheet of crisp white
computer paper. Aaron had printed those pages just for him, love for
a three-year-old in the most sacred sense.

When dinner was ready, we pushed ourselves in close around the
little dining table piled with vegetarian shepherd's pie and salad, and
challah bread that was still steaming warm. Because there were so
many of us, we ate at the couches, our drinks sitting on the coffee
table in the middle of all of us. Leanna and Aaron's little living room
was filled with the spirit of companionship, with the warmth of food
and family.

Leanna read a Sabbath prayer, broke the bread, passed it, and began
the Shabbat-Shalom celebration. We each turned to each other, gave
the *peace to you* greeting, saying with our eyes how thankful we are for
community, for freshness of spirit, for celebration of God seeing our
humanity.

We sat on the couches with our plates full, our wine glasses brim-
ming, laughing big, bellowing laughs. Leanna, our graceful host,

smiled all night, her entire being alight at the sound and sight of Sabbath celebration in her one-bedroom apartment.

We finished the meal, and I met Leanna in the kitchen to serve up the peach cobbler and vanilla ice cream in blue teacups. We stood working, not looking at each other. I told her I knew they would be leaving soon, moving away to a fresh season of God's grace starting seminary in another town, and that I'd miss her.

Sometimes community is made up of deep sorrow and deep joy all at once, and that is what Sabbath seems to echo. Shalom is a pronouncement of peace, of knowing that we are broken and filled with grief, but that we are also beckoned into deep joy.

Rest—Sabbath rest, communion rest—happens when we gather with each other and say our prayers of hope, our prayers of gratefulness, and our prayers of bare dependence upon God for every good thing.

Sabbath is for toddlers to climb on our knees to read books and laugh. It is for Aaron to pull out his trumpet after so many years and play it because Eliot asked him to.

It's the celebration-hurt of saying good-bye.

It is a late-night gathering of community with friends, new and old. It's the deep laugh of recognizing that life is good and holy, even when it's broken and messy.

That is Sabbath. That is shalom.

Jesus,
We are weak and shallow-hearted.
Yet, you give us your presence,
a deep well of kindness,
ever-flowing,
never ceasing,
to beckon us
to life
and breath.
We are shallow-hearted,
and yet,
we are placed within your care.
We are shallow-hearted,
and yet,
you call us into holiness,
deep and flowing and good,
and we find ourselves
allowed into a deeper
kind of living
than we've ever
known before.
Hallelujah.

8. STORYBOOK SPACES

When I speak of God, I mean this kind of love, this great yes to belonging.
—DAVID STEINDL-RAST[12]

R yan told us that we should invest in a Kindle or two as he heaved boxes and boxes of books up the stairs to our second-floor apartment.

We'd just arrived in Georgia, and the bulk of our belongings was books, our constant treasure.

Everywhere we move, our books go with us, carrying a world within our own, a separate world yet to be discovered.

When Travis, the boys, and I are on our beds or balled up at the corner of the couch with a blanket and a cup of coffee, our favorite words pour over us in a kind of baptism.

Eliot's first book was *Doggies* by Sandra Boynton. After a few months it fell apart at the binding from all the love it had received. He toted it with him everywhere, barked along to every page, and at the finale, howled with the *nine dogs on a moonlit night,* his head pointed toward that glowing orb above our house.

Before Isaiah was born, Eliot and I would pile books on the bed and read all of them through at bedtime, fifteen or twenty at once, and it was our favorite part of the day, the deep inhale and exhale after hours of work.

Now that Isaiah is a toddler, he has learned how to love these little portable worlds as well. We read *Brown Bear, Brown Bear, What Do You See?*, and he knows all the words on all the pages. Something about that repetition gives safety to a toddler, reminds them that they are loved and secure, that there is a big, wide world for them to enter into anytime they are so inclined.

We have *popcorn and poetry*—twenty minutes reading A. A. Milne and Robert Frost while we eat homemade popcorn sprinkled with sugar—and it is our favorite part of the afternoon.

In that stillness of book reading, we learn about the world through cardboard pages and typed words, through a stomping elephant or crawling spider. We sing the songs and we laugh over the ironies, and we expand our home, its walls bursting open for us to travel and trek into new spaces of pure pleasure and celebrated curiosity.

A world of reading brings a bounty far beyond us, and we find it creates a legacy to stretch far past us into every next generation.

But the best glory may be in what reading brings not just to the toddler, but to the mother who reads the words over and over and over again, who learns to love word and page again, who howls all the howls and remembers what it means to be moved by the pulse of a poem, who reawakens something long lost in the deeply broken world around her.

Jesus, give us yourself.
Give us your glory, the Kingdom promised in your
    blood and sweat.
Don't leave us alone and lonely, afraid and beguiled.
Gather yourself into the corners of our homes,
into the spaces we inhabit every day,
in the storybook reading and the
journal writing,
into the creating
and processing
and remembering,
the journeying.
Redeem us, restore us,
make our blood run clean in our veins,
so that we may remember how good it is to be
    together.
Glory and Hallelujah, we wait for you.
Amen.

9. THE MYSTIC

The fairest thing we can experience is the mysterious. It is the fundamental emotion which stands at the cradle of true art and true science. He who knows it not and can no longer wonder, no longer feel amazement, is as good as dead, a snuffed-out candle. —ALBERT EINSTEIN[13]

Travis asked me who I was as I stood over my balcony flowers and tended to their dead leaves. The vision was so foreign to him, both of us perplexed by the changes taking place in my thoughts and actions.

"I can't say right now," I replied. "All that I know is this experience I have with myself and with God, and there are no words for it."

We married when I was nineteen and he was twenty-one years young, and during the first year of our marriage we grew zinnias on the side of our one-bedroom house, a perfect patch of sunshine right outside the kitchen window. We had a tiny oak table planted right by that window where we ate our breakfast and drank our coffee, and I could look outside.

We dug little holes and planted the seeds, and I tried to appreciate digging my hands in that brown soil, but it was a struggle.

Seven years later, every tiny green head rising out of the pot on my balcony is a reminder of God in my midst, God bringing life-mystery to our tiny spaces.

Richard Rohr describes a mystic as "one who has moved from mere belief systems or belonging systems to actual inner experience."[14]

There, I thought, *it says it, so I must claim it: I'm a mystic in my searching.*

I've lived twenty-seven years and deeply loved the pictures of Jesus I've known, and always felt his kindness over me.

Now all I know is that it is somehow bigger.

This capacity to love is multiplied, and Jesus holds more than I ever thought, loves better than I've ever even wanted to love. He sees more than I'll ever see, and he asks me to marvel while he sits right next to me, reminding me that he is present and good.

I see that there are more facets to his being than we ever give him credit for, and that if we want to see them, it's going to take a great deal of time and vulnerability, a great deal of searching the open land of our hearts. His capacity for loving me will never be shaken as I search the wrinkle lines of his face, as I touch the palms of his rough carpenter hands.

When my father left when I was nine, my God was a fathering God, a parenting God, one who takes space in my home, in my surroundings, in my everyday experience. I knew the God of the Southern Baptist tradition and the God of the nondenominational church, and then the God of my Native American ancestors, all speaking to me—still.

The image has transformed through the years of my life, and today I see this Mysterious and benevolent good, and words can't quite make out a shape of what God means to me from day to day. And so the Mystery stretches into new forms and new shapes, into the quiet of an afternoon, into the laughter of my boys as they run barefoot on fluffy green grass.

And I see it in my friends, in my community, in my family, the ways that God injects Mystery into our lives and we cannot look away. There is so much good, unfathomable good, that we are undone by it.

And that's exactly where we are asked to be, to receive without understanding, to receive and know that it is good.

Because Jesus was human, his love knows our humanity, too. Jesus was marked for his work, for his kind doings, for his unmoving spirit, for his holy goodness.

If I am marked as a mystic today, may it be so, if only I am brought deeper in. There are no words to describe the deep love, all-encompassing, that searches our hearts. May our experiences bring us into glory on a daily basis and give us space to learn. May we only seek it, ask it, beg for it with our arms stretched toward Kingdom.

Tender Mystery,
Sometimes you slowly speak, small bits and pieces
    we try to work together
to see what's bigger there.
And then you stir wildly
and every emotional capacity is taken up,
every nerve pointed to your voice,
to the waiting,
to this severe need to be
close enough to hear you.
Speak.
Speak of the world to us.
You are the wildest and holiest experience.
You are the greatest adventure.
You are the best miracle-maker.
You are the truest lover.
Your voice echoes inside of us,
digs its way into our bones and veins,
our senses and brains,
into the most hollow corners,
into the darkest spaces.
Oh, you fill us.
Fill us again and again,
in every experience, glory abounding.
Amen.

10. THE EDGE

Self-care is not selfish or self-indulgent. We cannot nurture others from a dry well. We need to take care of our own needs first, then we can give from our surplus, our abundance. —JENNIFER LOUDON[15]

One day not long ago, I came to the end of myself.

I stood at the sink, where I always seem to find the awareness of my humanity as if I'm staring in a mirror, coming to my senses.

I stood at the sink, broken by my brokenness, unable to understand it.

I was overwhelmed by parenthood, overwhelmed by the work of mothering and pouring out, overwhelmed by trying to figure out how to parent patiently.

I was trying to break my selfish streak as best I could.

There at the edge of ourselves where we feel there's nothing to fix or redeem us—there—all we need is a gift.

We need a gift of grace, a gift of kindness, of someone seeing and understanding, someone saying *you're not alone.*

I opened *The Beauty of Grace,* a book of essays collected by my friend Dawn Camp. I was hungry for a voice to pull the tears from me, to give me permission to admit how hard it is to be a mother. Edie Wadsworth says it like this:

We don't have to try to be poor in spirit to receive His kingdom. We are poor in spirit, and we must beg Him to show us our emptiness in order that He may fill us with the bounty from His table. Everything is His. And so everything is yours.[16]

Edie writes that knowing our own poverty of heart allows us to be honest with ourselves and with God.

So, I let it all spill from me:

My poverty is my impatience.
My poverty is my pride.
My poverty is my envy.
My poverty is mistrust.
My poverty is fear.
My poverty is my own skin—
my loathing for it,
and yet, there is a table of bounty,
where I am welcomed in.
And so now, I lay bare my heart,
and I admit all of my poverties,
and I beg for the gift of salvation
to pull me away from the edge,
back to safety and quiet,
back to the hospitality of God.
Hallelujah and Amen.

And I stood up from the black loveseat in the sunroom and returned to the work of my day, back to the spaces that I inhabit, back to those holy spaces that inhabit me.

Holy Trinity,
You are the constant
in our wavering.
You are the always,
the always good.
May our hearts
learn to cherish
you.
Amen.

11. RUMMY

I want my boys to love Sunday, to find it a peaceful, pleasant day, when they can rest from common study and play, yet enjoy quiet pleasures and learn in simple ways, lessons more important than any taught in school.
—LOUISA MAY ALCOTT, *LITTLE MEN* [17]

When we were in Uganda in 2009 for two months, we lived on a compound with another team of Americans for a while. When the day was done, or there was an afternoon lull, we would all gather around a little table in the compound's front room and play an extremely competitive game of rummy.

It was Travis and me, the two Midwesterners in the room, and a group of California academics. It became our bond over those few weeks, and when we said good-bye, we vowed to play again, should we ever inhabit the same space.

When Travis and I moved to Arkansas so that he could start graduate school, we moved into a little three-bedroom home, newly renovated and beautiful. And because we weren't enrolled in school yet, we were living off of my Pier 1 Imports part-time salary until the fall.

We had no money.

And so, we played rummy. We tried Yahtzee, and after a few weeks threw the dice in the backyard for all the marital strife it caused. Rummy was our safe place, and so we played for hours a day.

We played when we were bored, we played while we ate dinner at the dining room table, and we played while we watched television. We played until our fingers were raw and our minds were numb, until we had to get out of the house and explore our new city.

This year at Christmas, we pulled out a few decks of cards from the china hutch at my in-laws, and we began again the beloved tradition.

We gathered at the dining room table, all of us at one end where we could fit chairs close enough to each other, and dealt the cards.

Home from our Christmas vacation, in the quiet of the afternoons when the boys were napping, Travis brought out that blue deck once again and we played for days in a row. Rummy has been with us for so many years and seems to return just when we need it.

Rummy was with us when we were newly married, barely a year in, scraping the Ugandan dirt-dust off the bottoms of our shoes. Rummy was with us after three years, when we had nothing but a dining room table, a beautiful little home, and our husky.

And Rummy is with us today, while the boys are in their own spaces and we have a few minutes to be together and sip our coffee and sweet tea.

When we keep a thing constant and let it stay with us for years and years, a tradition is made.

And when traditions are made, something happens in the way we come together, the way we stabilize ourselves and commit to each other, the way we make family.

One day the four of us will play, and our boys will beat us at every hand because they will be far cleverer than we. We will sit around the table and laugh and compete and know that safety and comfort can come by way of a blue deck of playing cards.

Jesus,
You give things to us that remind us of who you are.
You give us the wind so that we can remember
how the Spirit moves and breathes always over and
around us.
You give us each other so that we remember what
   your face
once looked like when you walked among us.
You give us light to remember who you've always
been.
And you give us tradition and togetherness
so that we can laugh and remember that while we're
human,
we can be human to and with
each other.
Amen.

12. *LE REPOSOIR*

We pass from thinking of God as part of our life to the realization that we are part of his life. —Richard Foster[18]

Our family joined the YMCA in our city a few months ago, because I've never consistently exercised in my life, and we want to begin habits of rest and health with our boys while they are young. So, on workout days, I drop them off with the other kids and go upstairs to the cardio area. I hop onto a stationary bike, and it is thirty minutes of release—thirty minutes of Balkan Beat Box playing in my earbuds and French scenery going by on the little screen in front of me.

I laugh a little to myself that I'm even in a gym, because I'm embarrassed that I only know how to use one machine in the whole place. But then I give thanks for the gym, and then I ask for more guidance and more light and more experience with these new practices that are becoming holy to me.

Riders can choose a route to cycle through, and I choose the winding French countryside. As I watch, I pray that I might see it in real life someday, might know more of this world that breathes Mystery into me.

The people around me are thinking their own thoughts, pondering God and relationships and health and how to make it from point A to point B.

In this society, women and men examine their bodies and health and try to understand what is or isn't enough, what might make them more perfect, or at least more acceptable. So this cardio area becomes a holy space, all these people sweating out their insecurities and bad choices, making way for endorphins and energy and space, making way for more life, one way or another.

I breathe with the pulse of the machine. I breathe as I lean over the handlebars and look at the timer and see that I have ten minutes left of this space. And I remember the people in my college tennis class who would laugh seeing me here today, because exercise then didn't mean what it means to me today, thirty minutes of kid-less quiet to examine who I am, what I give to them, what I need from this world, and what I owe to it.

I look up at the French countryside again, and the caption reads, "*Le Reposoir*"—the resting place. Until the day my family walks that countryside, knows that village's face and characteristics, speaks some broken French, and makes a friend or two as we pass through—until then, nothing could be more perfect for this season, more exactly true to what this stationary bicycle is to me on a Wednesday morning at the neighborhood YMCA.

Jesus,
I think we've gotten it wrong
again and again,
because we say
we know how and where
and when to find rest
and truth
and peace.
But then,
you surprise us
again.
You say, "No, not there."
"It's over here, and it's
waiting for you."
And then, if we get the chance
to open our eyes and see it,
we understand that
all this light is found
where you are,
everywhere and
anywhere
and in all those hidden
places
in
between.

And I think how lucky
we must be
to have someone who
loves us so much,
who is so full
of surprises
and goodness.
Thank you
for righting
our wrong,
for showing up
where we didn't
know you could.
Amen.

13. THE CAVE

The past is our definition. We may strive with good reason to escape it, or to escape what is bad in it. But we will escape it only by adding something better to it. —WENDELL BERRY[19]

When I was in fourth grade, we had a science unit on nature, and we chose to transform our classroom into a cave—making papier-mâché stalagmites and stalactites, cutting and gluing and painting after school.

Because there was no view from the windows in our small classroom, someone had painted an outdoor scene on one of the glass windowpanes, so that instead of seeing bricks from the classroom wall beside us, we saw rolling hills and sunbeams. We treasured that scene because it brought us peace in our little fourth-grade hearts.

That year my parents divorced, and that little room became a second home, a haven—from the early morning bell well into the afternoon hours. I would have been content to stay in that classroom with my teacher, Ms. DeGruson, instead of playing with the other kids at recess.

She was exactly the person I needed to care for me in one of the most volatile seasons of my life. She created a sanctuary for me in every sense of the word. After school, a small group of us would work on that cave project together, cutting and pasting, brainstorming and dreaming. I lived a few blocks away from the school, so walking home was easy enough, and I stayed as late as I could.

I loved the darkness overtaking our room, the beautiful gloom that only a cave can give. We worked so carefully, making sure every inch was covered with care. Day by day we worked until the cave was complete, until everything was in its proper place and all was black and brown.

And it's still there, deep in the folds of my memory, the place I rested during that long winter storm, a distant home.

Now, I sit on my balcony, rearranged every few months from the inspiration of a picture in a *Better Homes and Gardens* magazine. I change the plants in pots on an old ironing board against the ledge. I water the lavender and basil; I seek out the perfect spot for fall and winter lettuces and kale, for carrot roots to dig themselves deep into the soil.

Maybe the cave in fourth grade taught me about finding a home in those unexpected places, about finding sanctuary in natural blessings, with the sunlight and the moonlight, with the loud and the quiet.

Maybe that cave taught me that the Mystery of God takes us in and shelters us when we least expect it and most need it, to stay alive and tethered to everything that is good.

Jesus,
You give us shelter,
usually when we least expect it.
You give us kindness,
usually when we most need it.
You give us grace,
always when we're most hungry,
and you find us,
always when we're most tired of hiding.
How could we say anything
but thank you?
Thank you,
kind Shelter,
great Kindness,
Light of grace,
the One who finds us.
Amen.

PART THREE:

Weight

EZEKIEL 10:4–5

Then the glory of the LORD rose up from the cherub to the threshold of the house; the house was filled with the cloud, and the court was full of the brightness of the glory of the LORD. The sound of the wings of the cherubim was heard as far as the outer court, like the voice of God Almighty when he speaks.

14. FATHERING

Healing may come through medicine, through prayer, through presence and scent and calming touch, or through the consecrating of the journey as holy, dignified, and not without purpose or grace. —RACHEL HELD EVANS[20]

*I*t's been said that our pain teaches us something, brings us to a new place where we find that we've grown somehow into a more mature version of ourselves.

One day when I was nine years old, my father gathered his clothes, pulled my brother Tyler and me into the garage, and quietly said that he'd be leaving for a while. And off he went, into the police car we'd seen him drive every day for as long as we'd been alive. He drove down the street and away from the duplex we'd called home for a short time.

I remember the day, and I remember tiny glimpses past that, snippets of time and short shocks of pain in my mother's and siblings' faces. I remember the moment we finally understood that he wasn't coming back.

One night I sat in my room and begged for tangible hands to hold me, for big arms to take my balled up form and keep me steady while the waves crashed about. Other nights I closed my eyes and tried to sleep, worrying about the health of my father, about his future, about his heart, his journey through a wilderness I could not understand.

Walt Whitman wrote, "Happiness, knowledge, not in another place, but this place—not for another hour, but this hour."[21]

I was nine, so I didn't understand the economics of what came after—that we had to move to another neighborhood because we couldn't afford the current one without his income; that my mother worried herself in and out of depression taking care of us; that our new landlord, George, looked after us in ways he didn't have to, because he saw our extreme need.

My happiness was in that time, though, despite my fatherlessness and the reality of the hard years in which we were embedded. My happiness was in finding myself taken care of. Because the day Dad left, God's shoulder leaned in closer to me—this Mystery-presence placed upon my head—the warmth of his fingertips imprinting a kind glory onto my being.

His father-scent became stronger, his essence more tangible. And every hour became *the* hour to trust, *the* hour to believe and remain close to his listening ears.

Years later when I was newly married and attending a conference in DC, God spoke something to me in the darkness of a hotel ballroom during the opening dinner for the weekend. We had a few moments of quiet reflection during which we were asked to listen. The phrase *your ear is near my mouth* echoed over and over until it buried itself deep inside me—a forever seed—and I remembered my dad and those moments of hurt that hadn't been thought of in a while.

Pain shows up when we least expect, and yet, so does God. We were to write words on a rock before us on the table, an Ebenezer, a carved spot on the timeline noting where we were in that particular season and place.

On the one side I wrote *ear*, and on the other, *mouth*.

I found that stone when we moved from Arkansas to Georgia, buried deep in a forgotten drawer. Today, it reminds me of that blue-skied afternoon when the father the world had given me left, and I was brought closer in to the Father, who created me with the tiny spiraling movements of his fingers, speaking comfort into the fatherlessness I'd journey into one day at the age of nine.

Jesus,
Thank you for the way you pour yourself into humanity,
straight into our bones,
into the marrow,
where we've tried to poison ourselves with grief.
You are all joy,
all wonder,
and all relief.
Jesus, thank you for the loud and the quiet,
the laughter and the sobs—
it all means that we are alive,
that your reality finds us.
And to be human is to know every limit,
to see ourselves stacked against those realities,
against every hard truth.
To be human is to be able to grasp hope,
to hold it tightly to the chest,
to let its nectar seep into our hearts
and give us peace.
Yes.
Thank you for our humanity.
Amen.

15. LABORING

Here is the world. Beautiful and terrible things will happen. Don't be afraid. —FREDERICK BUECHNER[22]

When I became pregnant with our first son, Eliot, there were a lot of unknowns floating around in the air as I learned what it's like to carry a life inside a womb for nine whole months. I experienced pain that I never had before, weariness, and fresh strength, often all within the same few hours.

I was in labor for more than twenty-four hours; my contractions were extra long and extra painful. We'd watch the monitor show the peak of each one, and Barb, my nurse, would look at me wide-eyed and wonder how my little body was holding all of it in.

Travis and I had taken a class on the Bradley Method—I learned breathing techniques to deal with the pain of each contraction, and he learned how to work with me, speaking some sort of encouraging word while he held my hand and rubbed my back, while he fed me ice chips in the few minutes of respite I had between each one.

We were told to embrace and envelop the pain, to treat it as something to work *with* instead of *against*. As a Western society, we are pretty uncomfortable with things that hurt, and we are pretty uncomfortable with the process of grief and longtime healing. Because we are so afraid, we avoid what's uncomfortable. We hide in our fear thinking that it's safer there, that it won't hurt so much.

During my contractions, I'd start the exercise breathing, Travis holding my hand all the way through, and I'd wake up a minute later. I had fallen asleep. Somehow, my body found its rhythm with the pain, and not long after, Eliot was born.

I think about what I missed out on as a child because I was afraid.

I was afraid of the unknown, afraid of the dark, afraid of going too high or too far, afraid of the water, afraid of adventure.

In labor, I wanted to find an emboldened woman, and through each contraction, I found her inch by inch, taking off the veils that had long concealed her face and mighty strength. After Eliot was born, I was someone new; I had shed off layers of fear and constraint. I understood that when I lean into pain and let it run its sacred and difficult course, it teaches me something.

But when we could be leaning into the pain, many of us instead distract ourselves so it cannot reach us. Years later we find that we are still processing those things we were afraid to say out loud or face in our deepest need.

That is where community comes in, where we gather around each other and tell our stories. You'll know my hurts, you'll know where my pain stems from, what happens when I'm tethered to my identity fully and wholly.

In labor, each contraction has a beginning and an end. But in life the process winds back and forth, down and around as you feel your way through whatever is contracting inside of you. If we remember the process, maybe healing will look different for us; and if we treat healing differently, maybe sooner or later we will come closer to a fullness in our living, closer to the fullness of God with us after the long hours of labor are done.

Jesus,
Surely, you knew pain.
Surely, you knew what it meant
to breathe in and out
and look fear in the eye
and say that you
were going to be stronger
in the end.
Surely you knew
what it would take
to give birth to
your own death,
to quiet your soul
after hours of hanging.
And surely you knew
that those days of pain
would birth you again
into life,
into this new form of yourself
that you'd been waiting for
for so long.
May we lean into
ourselves that way,
leaning into you,

into the process of being human
and understanding our pain
as though it has something
important to teach us.
Lean us into our pain,
lean us into our strength,
lean us into
spirit
and soul
and life.
Lean us into you.
Amen.

16. IN TIMES OF EXPECTATION

So prayer is our sometimes real selves trying to communicate with the Real, with Truth, with the Light. —ANNE LAMOTT[23]

I was a few months pregnant with Isaiah when Travis, Eliot, and I flew to DC for a weekend conference on prayer and justice with International Justice Mission, an organization that fights global issues of modern-day slavery. I gathered myself together, told myself I could do it, that I wouldn't get sick on the plane, that my pregnancy-inspired hormones wouldn't claim another weekend of my life.

I'd gotten a pedicure, a haircut, and a spray tan. I'd bought a new outfit and prepared my heart for a sacred weekend.

Instead of pregnancy nausea claiming my time, I spent the entire three days in bed with the flu. I stepped into one session of the prayer conference, just long enough to sing as loud as I could with the worshipers around me. I needed it; I ached for it. I spent the entire weekend emotionally wrecked because I'd missed out on a trip I was looking forward to desperately.

Flying home on the plane, I tried to process what had gone wrong that weekend—how I could have missed out on the highlight of my year. I nursed Eliot to sleep and stared at my journal, but it was too raw, the grief settling in, the questions trying to ask themselves to the God I trusted, but didn't always understand.

I look at those pages and still can't find words for it, still can't find the courage to ask God exactly why it all happened that way, why a flu bug took over such an important weekend in my life.

A few months later, we spent a few weeks with my husband's parents. I had dreamt of spending time with Brenda, my mother-in-law, shopping at Goodwill and antique shops, laughing and cooking and celebrating the ever-forming boy in my belly. But when we arrived Brenda had to leave suddenly to visit her ill sister, and I was alone with Travis, his dad, toddler Eliot, and little Isaiah growing inside my tummy.

In the mornings, I was alone with Eliot while Travis and Micheal taught a class at the college.

While Eliot played, I looked around their library of a house—the walls lined with books—and remembered this hunger that had begun rooting itself in me to hear more from God, to lean closer and know more of that good comfort.

I chose Ann Voskamp's *One Thousand Gifts,* and I devoured it because it was about being thankful when things are not as they should be, about finding glory in unexpected places—like a weekend lost to the flu.

I sat in that living room, curled up on the pale green chair I can fold myself up inside of, pregnant belly and all. I took a notebook and filled it with notes, trying to process, trying to take the pieces and fit them back together again in a way that made sense.

I couldn't see anything ahead of me, and my present situation felt collapsed and unfruitful. I was begging for presence and purpose, for understanding. Because my heart is like a child's, the broken expectations weighed on me like a ton of bricks and felt unbearable.

I was swept back into long years of unmet expectations, promised visits with my father who didn't show up, promises broken once and broken again. After all that breaking, when a new joyfully expected thing goes awry, it weighs heavy on a heart.

I found Ann's book again a few years later in our little apartment, and saw all the notes I'd scribbled in it. I was so hungry then, so ready and waiting for truth.

I'm still hungry today, hungry again for God's voice in my child-like waiting and expecting. And all I can do is acknowledge that a mysterious and good presence held me in that earlier season, and that it filled me, despite the broken expectations and the tiredness in my heart.

When we are tired and hungry, the Mystery of God is still present after all. That tiny but constant voice still echoes in hotel rooms and big library-houses.

That voice still echoes in all of us, when tears fill our eyes, when we're begging for breath all over again. It still beckons glorious kindness to enter in and make a home within those hollow spaces.

I have discovered you, and I am discovering you.
In the watchful hours of night, I watch my little one and
    you watch me.
In the bright light hours of day, we play, all of us,
and work and toil, back into the waxing moon's shadow.
And there we quiet down again.
And there we are discovered,
and there we discover.
I am discovering you, Being all-knowing,
who seems to give all to me.
You are Giver and Bringer and All in One.
Treasure and surprises seek me out when I am most
    unseekable.
You seek me, find me, pour me out and fill me again.
May we discover, and in discovering, find the healing of
    ages.
May we discover Kingdom come, Kingdom coming,
Kingdom forever and always and into every horizon
    we've yet to unearth.
May we discover the journey of discovering all of you,
    all the beauties of you
and depths in you and widths bounding through you.
Beckon us to you, sacredness in the path
beneath our tired, anxious feet.

And rest us at the edges of ourselves,
the unexpected places,
where horizon meets holy horizon
   and we are bound by no shame,
covered by no fear.
Amen.

17. TRANSFUSION

Like any true mirror, the gaze of God receives us exactly as we are, without judgment or distortion, subtraction or addition. Such perfect receiving is what transforms us. —RICHARD ROHR[24]

I still have two little slits of a scar on my left forearm where they cut my skin when I was eleven and waited for the blood to clot. It took much longer than it should have. They thought it was leukemia, but it wasn't. Later that day, at that hospital in St. Joseph, Missouri, I had a blood transfusion, which confirmed that my blood isn't normal. It is a blood disorder that would come and go throughout my life, causing my blood to cease clotting. I returned home to my brother, sister, and other friends and family, and they gathered around me and loved me in my paper-thin, china-doll state.

My sister, Tiffany, is nine years older than me, and when I was young I spent most of my time with her and her college friends. When I joined them at the Koinonia college ministry that met in the sanctuary of College Heights Christian Church, I stood in the pew and worshiped in a way I'd never been able to before.

Tiffany lived with a few roommates at the Girls' House, and right down the street on the corner was the Guys' House, where we played soccer in the yard and video games in the living room. I spent a lot of time in the backyard of her house. A hammock swing hung down from the giant tree off to the side of the back porch, and I'd pivot back and forth, listening to Nicole C. Mullins and singing at the top of my lungs to anyone who might be listening, a worship event for all to join.

I loaded and unloaded their dishwasher, ate their food, and watched their movies. All that I knew was that these people took me in as their little sister, and after the transfusion, more love seemed to pour out over me. I remember Dusty, Jackson, Josh and Jay, Trisha and Charity, Bethany and her brother Brandon. I remember the way they laughed with me, invited me to come along, honored my young girl's worshipful heart.

One night, after I'd mostly recovered from the hospital stay, I packed my bag to spend the night with my sister and her friends. The weakness in my body must have shown through on my face, because everyone was extra sensitive toward me that night, helping me up and down, watching me as I rested in the corner of the room, entertaining me as best they could.

As a preteen trying to find her way in a frail and broken and beautiful world, they were the best friends I could have imagined for myself. All I needed was to be a part of them.

From their friendship, I learned friendship myself.

I learned what it means to serve and care for someone, what it means to live in community and walk side by side. I learned that it's possible to find a best friend in a sister. I learned that a blood transfusion is just one more reason to dig in roots and stay connected to the people who love you deeply, who take you, tired skin and bones, ragged soul, and all.

O God,
We pray for ourselves, for our children,
for our friends, that we find
community, people whom we need
at the right time and in the right way.
But whether we pray it or not,
I think you've already got that in mind
for us.
You birth us into the world
with community in mind,
and when we are in so much need
of someone, you seem to call
us back to you through the people
who love us well and wholly.
And when we are afraid
or fragile or broken or simply undone,
you meet us with human
face and hands, flesh and heart,
to hold us there and remind us
that we are not alone.
Hallelujah, we are not
alone.
Amen.

18. GADY

Every happiness is a bright ray between shadows, every gaiety bracketed by grief. —GERALDINE BROOKS[25]

I first encountered someone in close relationship with cancer on a mission trip with the Forest Park Baptist Church youth group one summer, when we were hosting VBS in a little church near a village dump in Mexico.

Gady was barely nine years old, and his father was the pastor. He'd just been diagnosed with leukemia. The summer before, he and I had played in the one-room church overlooking a dirt field where the kids kicked a soccer ball every day. Gady was our little brother—this boy so full of life and mischief, so kind and honoring to his mother and father.

We worked in that same town over the next few summers, but as Gady got worse, we weren't able to continue work at their small church. Still, we would visit him while we were there. Once during our evening prayers and worship, we decided to gather money late in the night to give to Gady's family to help cover their expenses. The next morning, we took the envelope to his house, three hundred and eighteen dollars, placed it in his father Jose's hands, and asked him to take it and let it be the grace of God for their family. We returned home knowing our arms couldn't possibly reach Gady as we carried on with our own lives; we couldn't do anything more than pray, and we carried his life story inside ourselves.

When I was in high school, my sister-in-law was diagnosed with cancer, and everything about it mirrored Gady for me, every prayer bouncing back and forth between the two of them, their stories and names engraved right next to each other in my heart. When I wrote *Melanie* in my prayers, *Gady* came next, a constant cycle of pleading and tears.

The year that Melanie passed away we visited Gady's family again on a summer trip in Mexico. He was too weak to walk—his body was failing him. His father was at the church next door, praying to God to lean in and teach him something in all of his sorrow.

When we got back to the church across town where we were working, I leaned against the door of the kitchen and cried harder than I'd cried in a long time. It was a deep ache and grief—intensified and made real for me through the lens of my own family's heartache in losing Melanie. The rest of that year back in the United States, I wore a bracelet with Gady's name spelled in beads threaded across my wrist. My prayers echoed each other—*Melanie, Gady—Gady, Melanie*—back and forth until the tears finally gave out and my eyes dried up again.

Two years later, Gady passed away. Lawrence, the man who led our trips in Mexico, e-mailed me the news the year that I was a freshman in college, about to get married. At the end of the e-mail, he wrote, "He will know you when he sees you in heaven." With everything in me, I ached for it to be true.

Death takes something from us and gives something to us. It adds to the tension of our lives, this Kingdom come but not yet coming that we endure while we still breathe. Gady and Melanie knew life and death, and I watched it in their eyes, had word of it from afar.

I pasted Gady's picture to my wall for years. I wrote a song about Melanie so that my grief would mean something to me, something to honor her memory and my stepbrother Heath's journey with her.

It is true that I prayed for healing for them both, that I prayed for restoration of Gady's tiny body, and for his heart and soul. It is true that I prayed for his wholeness, for his family to find peace.

But I also prayed that God would teach me something in the suffering, that I would learn to walk closer to the line between life and death, that I would see the face of death differently, that I would let something holy come from the pain that cancer brings—from all the pain surrounding human suffering.

I don't understand how that works, but Melanie and Gady are both engraved deep into my being, their names still spoken every now and then in a prayer, their souls still whispering into the air what it means to live and die and live again, what it means to give up something of earth to find something unearthly, something holier than what I will ever know here in this skin.

And I pray with everything that I am that when I see them in that new form, their arms will spread wide and they will know me, see me, greet me with a holy kiss and an embrace, that we will gather together there and say, *We lived, didn't we? We lived and died and it was all called good in the end. We lived and died and lived again, God's grace abounding. Hallelujah.*

O God of grace,
We've been told of heaven our whole lives,
told of this sacred place,
all whitewashed and clean,
all choir robes and tables
full of plump grapes and ham
and maybe a little wine, but probably
just grape juice.
We've been told that, there, we won't hurt anymore.
We've been told that our bodies look different
and new, that our scars disappear once we
pass through that pearly gate.
I hope for it,
but I also hope that we look just like we do here,
that we see some of our scars
so that we can remember who we were
and who we are
and who we will be.
I hope there's more than just white,
that we wear the colors of the rainbow and
colors that we didn't even know existed,
that we get to experience life in every sense
of fullness we never knew we could.
I hope that heaven gives us all of you,

your presence so near to us that we can
smell you
and hug you
and know that you are so near.
And I pray that when we see each other,
those people we've spent our lives with,
that we can touch each other's scars
and look in each other's eyes
and know that you've wanted us all along,
the broken and unbroken parts,
clean and unclean,
wrecked and restored,
before and after,
with and without grace.
You wanted us before we knew you,
and I pray that heaven will show us
that you want us forevermore.
Amen.

19. HUNGER

It is better to sleep with an empty stomach than a troubled heart.
—UGANDAN PROVERB

One day we were driving home from grocery shopping at lunch time, and the boys and I were all feeling it, the intense hunger that hits around eleven in the morning and again around dinnertime at five.

I had to consciously make a decision to listen—this time—before we all became irate.

Because we are so well fed, so taken care of, we don't handle our hunger well. But what if we actually choose to *listen to it, not just the rumbling in our stomachs but the ache in our hearts?*

What if we let that be our metaphor?

If our hunger is telling us our need, maybe there is an internal hunger reminding us that our heart is longing to be fed, too. So that day, I tried to listen to the heart-hunger instead.

For years, we've prayed at the table; we've given thanks for the bounty before us, for the meal prepared and the hands that curated it. But if we listen to our hunger, we listen to the heartbeat of so much of the rest of the world. And if we hear the pain of the world, we remember that Jesus always gives us just what we need.

And so, Eliot prays, "Jesus, thank you for the Spirit, and we love God when we hear him in our hearts."

And Isaiah says, "Jesus . . . Rhoda," and prays for his favorite cousin.

And we take those first few bites of protein, breathe deep, and remember that we are cared for.

When we listen to our hunger, we give light to the reality that we're not quite as we should be, that Kingdom comes but still keeps coming.

Every single day.

Until one day the hunger will cease for everyone.

"We're learning to breathe these days. That's the gift of the Spirit," my friend Devita said as she preached at my church one Sunday. If we listen closely, there's a gift in our hunger, a gift that we release when we take the bread and drink from the sippy cup or the coffee mug.

We stop and breathe and say, "Spirit. Thank you for your slow and steady work. Fill my hungering parts."

Amen and amen, for constant, filling, holy presence.

Hallelujah, that our hunger reminds us.

Holy Spirit,
When you poured out your breath on the church,
    you changed everything—again.
Jesus had undone so many,
had reversed and rewritten the laws of men and
    women,
and then he was gone, and maybe everyone thought
that it would be quiet for a while.
But then you brought new languages to their lips,
a new birth into community,
into the church,
a new realm of God come to earth.
And maybe there they saw their own hunger,
just as we do today.
Maybe there, they saw Jesus again in your kind and
    wild presence.
Maybe there, they believed in Kingdom reality
    forevermore.
May we believe, even now.
Amen.

PART FOUR:

Voice

DEUTERONOMY 5:24

Look, the LORD our God has shown us his glory and greatness, and we have heard his voice out of the fire. Today we have seen that God may speak to someone and the person may still live.

20. ISAIAH DESMOND

Life is either a daring adventure or nothing. —Helen Keller[26]

he day Isaiah was born, I told Travis to pack a few of my favorite books for the hospital. One was *Yours Is the Day, Lord, Yours Is the Night,* a compilation of prayers by Jeanie and David Gushee.

When Isaiah was born forty minutes after we arrived, I asked Travis to read the prayer for August 26 over him, praying that the kindness of God would bring a life of justice and peacemaking to him on the celebration of his birthday.

The ancient Welsh prayer reads:

> *Grant, O God, your protection:*
> *and in your protection, strength;*
> *and in strength, understanding;*
> *and in understanding, knowledge;*
> *and in knowledge, the knowledge of justice;*
> *and in the knowledge of justice, the love of it;*
> *and in that love, the love of existence;*
> *and in the love of all existence, the love of God,*
> *God and all goodness.*
> *Amen.[27]*

We took Isaiah in our arms and spoke over him, covering him in a tiny infant-sized glory cloud of promise.

The words on the page brought forth holiness and poured it into the heart of a newborn boy, the boy who was born two days before his actual due date.

Eleven months after Isaiah was born, we moved to Georgia, and found ourselves in the same community as David and Jeanie, the people whose collected prayers ushered me into God's presence time and again. I dreamt of the day I'd meet them, of the day I could stand in front of them and explain that God speaks through books filled with prayers. I couldn't wait to tell them that my son was called into being with those words two days before his due date, called into the Mystery that first breathed life into his tiniest parts.

We sat at David and Jeanie's table eating bowls of chili one evening, and I watched them talk to my boys, embrace them and call them blessed. I heard Eliot call him *Professor David* in that toddler voice, with a heart that claimed these two people as his own flesh and blood. And I thought back across this journey, the steps that took us from that Arkansas hospital to their Atlanta home where we sat, blanketed in thanksgiving for the way God speaks life over all of us.

A month before Isaiah's second birthday, Travis went away for ten days to teach a summer class at Duke in North Carolina. The night he came home, he spread his arms straight out to the left and the right, revealing a tattoo of the very same prayer we'd read over Isaiah's baby body the day he was born.

We proclaimed it there again, with the words forever engraved on his father's arms, the story of who Isaiah Desmond was always supposed to be, someone who forever knows the essence of *God and all goodness,* who pours life into him daily.

O God,
Where we gather,
the ceiling settles down, walls bring themselves close,
and we are pressed into one another,
all messes and mishaps, all brokenness in the midst
  of praise.
So, lead us toward one another.
May we look each other in the eyes,
and heal each other's blindness.
May your blood seal us into each other,
so that we may not escape one another—
so that we may not escape you.
Because when you hemmed us in,
it was all of us, together,
forever bound and held
in you.
There is our Hallelujah,
and there is our Amen.

21. THE STORY PEOPLE

Whether alone or among people, we always carry with us a portable sanctuary of the heart. —RICHARD FOSTER[28]

*J*ared and Lindi invited us to their house for a get-together of close friends, and we were excited, but a little stumped. People we'd only known for a few weeks were bringing us in and covering us in hospitality, but we weren't sure why. When Lindi announced that she was pregnant, we all cried, and Travis and I got in the car saying *these people will be our people for a long time.*

The next week, we found out that I was pregnant. We drove to Mama Carmen's coffee shop where Lindi worked to see her and Jared. They looked at us for a few seconds, and knew. We laughed and cried and it hit us again. *These people will be our people.*

Jared and Lindi brought us into a community of Christ-seeking, love-abiding sinners who drank in the Spirit of God in all ways they could muster. Our first evening with this group, I walked into the kitchen and met our new friends. Amber was pregnant and excused herself for looking so big and round; I thought she was the prettiest and sweetest thing I'd seen in a long time. Lindsey had just had Nora, and brought us into her home with such grace and warmth, I could barely contain my emotion.

We were home.

It was a gathering of mamas in all shapes and sizes, of dads and dads-to-be seeking companions for the long journey. We spent nights in worship, our group growing bigger and bigger as the weeks went by, filling up with college students and young professionals who longed for more connection.

We laid hands on each other, prayed for life and truth. We sang over each other as our boys got bigger and bigger and we dealt with health scares and passing due dates. We all struggled to know each other and to know God, because we were safe to struggle there. It was organic living in every sense, the most native of all kinds, where the bond of Christ starts at the root and blooms into fragrant, fruitful worship.

Joseph and Lindsey welcomed us again and again into their kitchen and backyard garden where tomatoes grew in abundance. We watched over each other. We prayed for each other. We remembered Christ's body and blood embodied in each other, a sacred and real-life glory.

One night at Seth and Amber's old stone house, we had a community group campout, people piled in every room, all across the living and dining room floors in sleeping bags, those with babies upstairs in beds. We sat in the living room, staring at the candles and pictures on the extra-large fireplace. We believed that to serve each other, we had to understand each other, to know the details of each other's lives so that the grace that was spread over us could continue to fill us, bring us closer in. We shared stories of who we were and how we'd come to be that way.

That night was story upon story, of fathers leaving their children or parents forever faithful, of the brokenness of the church and the holiness of it. There was laughter and tears, with steaming coffee and warm potluck food.

Barbara Brown Taylor said, "At the very least, most of us need someone to tell our stories to. At a deeper level, most of us need someone to help us forget ourselves, a little or a lot."[29]

Not long after that night, our community group, which had built up to an average of more than fifty people per week, decided to *branch off* because *splitting up* sounded too painful. We divided up into smaller groups, still staying tethered to each other, to our stories, to what had happened there.

In those short two years, I didn't see the fruit that was being born in me, but today I recognize the grace in all of it. I long for that season of community before the branching, a vision of Kingdom on earth, a picture of Kingdom to come.

The reality is, there are people all over, in every season, who can be our people, if we only stop and look, if we only listen and share and understand that loving community takes time and starts as a seed in the heart, just like it took a year for us to find Jared and Lindi, Joseph and Lindsey, Seth and Amber.

And the Spirit spreads from there. Glory finds us once again, and God calls humanity to himself in the face of every joy and pain, in the face of the church and all that she embodies in a community of worshipers and storytellers.

Holy Spirit,
We are so thankful that you are
a world without end.
We see things so presently, so daily,
so small and abrupt.
But your sight stretches,
your goodness covers us,
covers our world.
Give us new eyes,
new hearts to see Kingdom things,
to take in Kingdom stories
and claim them as our own,
because they belong to our humanness.
May we stretch ourselves,
not into unneeded brokenness,
but into you,
where unspoken words are heard,
where wounds are healed,
where we find that
we are part of eternal things,
even here on earth.
Hallelujah that you invite us in.
Amen.

22. SEEDLINGS

The place God calls you to is the place where your deep gladness and the world's deep hunger meet. —FREDERICK BUECHNER[30]

Eliot has been talking to our seeds.

The Georgia sun stays active all year long, and you can feel her presence in the middle of a winter day. She comes to you, streaming through the open blinds, giving nourishment to the grass on the lawn, and calling water up through the roots of every living plant.

When spring turned warm enough, we drove to Lowe's and stocked up on little seed bags and potting mix. We spent an entire afternoon digging into the dirt on our city balcony.

Now Eliot leans in real close and whispers in his high-pitched, talking-to-a-baby voice, "How are you, seeds?" Then he sits up, looks at me, and says, "They are good."

Maybe it's just an old tale that says talking to flowers will actually help them grow, but I think it does us some good anyway, to consider that those herb seeds might be listening and that we might need a friend.

And sure enough, we've seen the green begin to stretch past pebbles of soil, reaching up for the sun, reaching up for that little voice calling them out of the darkness. The sunflowers have reached up to their second leaves, have started to form their bulky stems. The dill is coming alive in its most delicate form; the cilantro is perched up, waxy and waiting.

And we tell them, "Just keep growing. Come and meet us. We are waiting for you." The boys sing songs about potting flowers; they sing about life coming up through the holes in the dirt they were just making with their fingers.

I took our linen, hanging shoe organizer from the closet door and put it outside, and planted seeds in its pockets. It was a community of little homes, where seedlings say hello, flowers and herbs tell us that they're alive and ready for more water, more voice.

And so it is with us, when we reach out of our own dust, when we finally long for the sun enough that we let God pull us into bright light, into communion and community.

The little voice of my toddler beckons those green fingers toward him, just as God gently leans in, asks how we're doing, and lets us climb up back toward him, back into the glorious light of day.

In the bright heat of summer, we shield our eyes and
    search the skies for you.
We dig in our garden dirt for your life,
your promise of nurture.
In the calm death of fall, we watch leaves ride on
    your wind,
watch animals sprint across roads and through acres
    of grass to fill up on life.
In the swallowing up of snowstorms in winter, we
    hide under covers,
we snuggle by fires to see that you still burn bright,
    you still reach us.
And in spring, you usher us back to life, beckon us to
    the sun
with mild blooms and glorious stretches
of hiking graveled paths and tasting rainwater.
We see, then, that you're there always, that you're
    here,
living and breathing over all of it.
May we know your world,
may we serve it and let it serve us,
all for the love of you.
Amen.

23. DARK GIVES LIGHT

I felt it shelter to speak to you. —EMILY DICKINSON[31]

*I*t was the middle of the afternoon. The boys were asleep, Travis was reading on the couch, and I sat, restlessly trying to make myself quiet and still.

Then, the deep beckoning.

This longing to shut myself up, to close off everything but coffee cup and candle flame and voice. Just the quiet of the soul and the listening ear of God. It was like Lizzie and Papa in Georgian England, the *Pride and Prejudice* duo huddled up in his study on a rainy day to discuss the dreaming of their hearts.

So I grab the purple candle in a blue teacup, I heat up my coffee, and I sneak in.

I close the closet door, and all that is left is the quiet heave of Isaiah's chest, breath-in-lungs, as he sleeps on my bed. What do you say when it's all quiet? What do you splutter into that darkness, that flickering flame and listening Spirit?

All I can give is thanks. All my breath, all my tired body can retrieve from my soul's mouth is a sighing gratitude.

I pray:

Thank you for open doors.
Thank you for a community of women.
Thank you for caring about me.
Thank you for wanting me.
Thank you for my husband, his deep and kind heart.
Thank you, thank you, thank you.

And I ask that Spirit to help me understand, to help me learn to love my boys better.

Help, help, help.

And I sit staring at the flame, at the coffee steam.

I wasn't sure what listening meant then, and I still don't know—I'm so often so bad at it.

Back in the closet, he so gently calls me to himself, to the quiet; all I can do is hasten and admit all my childlikeness.

And I whisper:

I trust you.

But, help me trust you.

Then, I breathe deep. Two deep breaths to remember his presence, to listen in.

I'm here, he says.

I really love you, I say. *But, help me love you.*

Breathe. Breathe.

I'm here, he says.

And then it ends.

I quietly sneak away, past the baby boy still fast asleep.

I go do the dishes, make bread, cuddle my other waking toddler.

The dark, the quiet, the flame—a few moments of fuel, a tiny sliver of Kingdom-to-person contact, the essence of Christ's love and faithfulness to every tired child, spoken from the darkness of a bedroom closet where light beckons me home.

Jesus,
When we return to our places,
to our routines and stresses
and everyday occurrences,
help us stay tethered.
Give us purpose, even through
the darkness of the long night.
Give us peace,
give us hope,
that everything stays illuminated
because you are fully life and fully light.
Amen.

24. LIVING PRAYERS

Take time to pray with your children in the morning. It has far more power for your family and your planet than all your busy work.
—DHYANI YWAHOO[32]

One afternoon, I cut some pieces of yarn and sliced an empty toilet paper roll into a few separate "beads" so that Eliot and Isaiah could make necklaces. They colored their thin circles of cardboard, and we strung them along the blue yarn and tied them at the end.

Eliot took off his necklace and kept it there at the table with him while he ate lunch.

"Mama," he said, "can this be like your necklace with the red beads that you hold in your hands and pray with? Can I hold these in my hands and pray with you?"

We do not understand how God's Spirit spreads itself inside of a child when we do our small part of mentioning that he loves them and that he's listening. I touched his cheek and said, "Yes, Baby, I would love for you to pray with me."

These are the spaces in which parenting becomes especially difficult: the follow-through. I'd had that rosary for a few weeks. I was still learning how to pray and when. I'm not very good at making that quiet space in the midst of my day.

We can tell our children all about God, but there are things we need to show them.

"Christianity is to have one's body shaped, one's habits determined, in a manner that the worship of God is unavoidable," Stanley Hauerwas said.[33]

We are shaped by our daily habits, by the way we pray in the light and in the dark, by the way we speak and the way we trust. We worship God in the way that we cry and scream and ask when we are uneasy, in the way we fully trust the Mystery to occupy our corrupt spaces and fill them with joy and fulfillment.

Eliot and I will learn to pray together, will learn to whisper to the light and to the darkness of glorious things, to celebrate the holy and triumphant things:

Glory be to the Father, and to the Son, and to the Holy Spirit.
As it was in the beginning, is now, and ever shall be,
World without end.
Amen.

I learn daily that if I selfishly guard all of my time, all of my habits, all of my chores, I will slowly separate myself from these two rowdy boys. They want to engage in my world; they want me to create a safe place for them to see God, to experience him, to worship him in every facet of their being.

Perhaps it starts with a rosary bead. Perhaps it starts with a tent and a flashlight. Perhaps a cut-apart toilet paper roll and a strand of yarn. Perhaps it's in the middle of the night, eating a snack at the kitchen table. Perhaps it's in my very breathing, in taking grace and speaking it back out, glory in all ways to the people I love.

Eliot prays before our meals, "God, thank you that you talk to us in our hearts."

I echo the thankful expression of Richard Rohr: "Prayer happened, and I was there."[34]

And my toddlers teach me how to speak it, how to hold the bead and remember the faith, and there we have all we need.

Jesus,
Maybe we learn to see you
when our little ones are doing crafts
    at the dining room table.
And maybe when we see their tiny hands
and their endless creativity
we are ushered back to our childlikeness,
and we find ourselves crawling back into your lap,
back into the comfort of your
embrace and the quiet of your soothing Papa voice.
May it be so.
Amen.

25. JOHN AND SUZAN

*It's been the plan all along, the call on every life—we are created beings
with the capacity to hold God.* —AMBER HAINES[35]

One weekend I went back to Missouri and Arkansas to visit
family and friends. The boys came along on their first big-
boy plane ride—a few hours across the South and Midwest,
licking orange and yellow lollipops, and coloring.

After a few days in Missouri with my family, I borrowed my sister's
car and headed through the Ozark Mountains back to Fayetteville,
where we had started our family a few years before. We drove straight
to Suzan's house, our former neighbor and great-grandma to the boys
in every sense but actual blood. She had taken Eliot on walks while
I was pregnant with Isaiah, spent the mornings examining trees and
digging up worms and socializing with all the other neighbors while
I rested on the couch and journaled. After Isaiah was born, she began
walking the two of them along with her friend Ruth and the two girls
she cared for like a grandmother, a little parade marching through our
tiny neighborhood.

And every time we go back now, there is no one else that they
want to see but Suzan, because my boys' Fayetteville world is
summed up in Suzan's backyard garden, in the tomato plant out
front and the crocuses that line the drive, in eating popsicles and
being spoiled by love and good food and movies and digging in every
spot of mud available.

So I left the boys with Suzan for an entire day and headed to Onyx
Coffee Lab, the coffee shop and roaster where Travis had worked as a
barista. I ordered my latte and nestled into the back bench. It was like
my whole being was laid wide open, ready to receive, an entire day to
rest and hear and know the presence of God in my midst.

Not long after, John walked in the door, this man that I'd always wanted more time with before we moved, a local pastor and community advocate. He is a father figure if ever there was one. I stood up and hugged him and felt the tension in my shoulders slacken under the weight of his pastoring love.

We had a short ten-minute conversation before he left to go cycling with a friend. It was the quickest conversation I had that entire weekend, but those few minutes filled me and sparked life in me and sent me off to find more of God, sent me on a search for new spaces inside of myself.

I told John about my dad leaving when I was young, something I wouldn't usually bring up after two minutes with someone. We talked about church and immediately walked into the heaviness of what it means to love people and be inclusive, what it means to ask questions and challenge others to walk more deeply with the Mystery of God.

When our conversation abruptly ended, I settled back into the booth. I could see in the eyes of the stranger across from me that something had come to life in her. Even in listening to a quick conversation between two friends, she understood something of God, something of community and human connection and companionship—all sacred and holy.

I spent all three mornings of our trip in that coffee shop, watching the front door open and close, watching it bring in old friends that I hadn't seen in a year or two. John and the other friends who came after him were balm to me, slight whispers to keep going, to keep processing and enduring, living a life called to wholeness and all glorious things. All the while, across town, my boys were with Suzan, learning the exact same thing.

O God,
Thank you for quiet conversations over coffee cups
and mugs of tea, for memories and new stories,
reminders that you find us and we find you
when we look into each other's eyes.
Thank you for these spaces.
We know that they are sacred because they give us
room to breathe,
to remember who we are,
to ask who we should be.
Thank you that
you honor all of it,
all of us,
all of these realms that
you call holy.
Amen.

PART FIVE:

Fire

2 CHRONICLES 7:1–3 (MSG)

When Solomon finished praying, a bolt of lightning out of heaven struck the Whole-Burnt-Offering and sacrifices and the Glory of GOD filled The Temple. The Glory was so dense that the priests couldn't get in—GOD so filled The Temple that there was no room for the priests! When all Israel saw the fire fall from heaven and the Glory of GOD fill The Temple, they fell on their knees, bowed their heads, and worshiped, thanking GOD:

Yes! God is good!

His love never quits!

26. SASHA

Wrong will be right, when Aslan comes in sight,
At the sound of his roar, sorrows will be no more,
When he bares his teeth, winter meets its death,
And when he shakes his mane, we shall have spring again.
—C. S. Lewis, *The Lion, the Witch and the Wardrobe*[36]

One rainy and cold January day we found a black Labrador retriever named Sasha wandering our apartment complex. Travis met her outside someone's door, shivering and wet, waiting for a friend to take her inside. The boys and I stood at the window and watched, and we couldn't *not take her,* keep her safe from the storm until her owners showed up to take her back.

So, we brought her home for the day.

All morning she ran around our apartment with Isaiah's blue ball, the one covered in the planets and solar system. Saturn would roll over and over on itself as Sasha played fetch with whoever would give her the playful attention she so desperately ached for.

I'd sit on the couch to read a book and feel a wet nose near my foot, two eyes looking up at me until I responded. She'd wrestle with Travis and lay down by our husky, Sam. Our hearts were full and overwhelmed by her sweet, independent spirit.

We took her outside to play in the giant snowflakes that fell for ten full minutes in the afternoon, she and Sam racing around the complex parking lot with white flecks on their fur.

"She was so sad, but now she has a family. I love her," Eliot said.

That evening, we found her owner, and as Travis buckled her leash onto her collar to walk her home, Isaiah wiped huge tears from his toddler cheeks. He told Sasha to keep his ball, to take it home to remember him by, but she dropped it at the door as if to say, "No, I'll remember today. I'll remember you without the keepsake."

That night the snow kept falling, the first snow of our Georgia winter. How young Sasha escaped from the apartment across the way is unclear, but everything else makes sense.

We needed some extra joy and magic on that first snow day. We needed a reason for celebration. Sam needed to be reminded of companionship, of how the pack works. I needed those little eyes begging me for attention, and our boys needed a youthful friend to sit by their side at rest time and pretend with them in their play kitchen.

Travis needed to spend time cuddling with this feisty Lab, to dream ahead to a day when we would be back in a house with a yard full of dirt and grass, a dog or two resting in the shade of an oak tree.

We needed Sasha that cold January day far more than she needed us, and every time Isaiah looks at that ball of his, he whispers her name and looks to the heavens with a nod and a word of thanks to the God who sees his every need, every single day.

Jesus,
There is magic in the first
winter snowstorm.
There is magic in those flakes,
in the shine of white
on the windowsill
and the cars parked outside.
For a little while
we do not worry,
because we are
in a cocoon of
white,
resting in the quiet
of our afternoon,
waiting for life to
come upon us
and ask us to step
out again and
engage the world outside.
And in that white snow-world,
we experience you.
We experience your magical
presence,
this thing we do not understand

but so long to know.
Indeed, with every season-miracle
we see you
and come to know you
a glimmer better,
and that is so full
of blessing
in itself that we are
overcome with gladness.
Thank you for the
magic.
Amen.

27. FULL CIRCLE

Ah, children . . . How good life is when you do something good and rightful! —FYODOR DOSTOEVSKY, *THE BROTHERS KARAMOZOV* [37]

Years ago when we first moved to the hills of Arkansas, our car was broken into.

We came home late from an out-of-town trip and we were exhausted; I accidentally left one car door unlocked with all of our belongings still inside. The next morning, the passenger door was wide open and everything was gone.

We lost many of our things, including our laptops and the Chacos Travis had strapped to his feet as he trekked across Bosnia and Uganda a few years before.

Three weeks later, we drove to Oklahoma to speak at Aaron and Nikki's church for a youth-group event. (My mom and Nikki's mom have been best friends my whole life, so going to Oklahoma is always going home.) We were giving a presentation on God's heart for social justice. I led worship and performed songs I'd written, and Travis gave the presentation.

Beforehand, Aaron explained to the teens that our talk would be a bit sparse, given we'd had no laptop to prepare it with. After the event, we spent the evening at Aaron and Nikki's house with their children and Nikki's mom, Karen. While we danced to Disney songs with their two daughters, Courtney and Andrew came over. We'd met them earlier that night; they had a mysterious and sweet presence about them. We sat around the table and had coffee and shared our vision for the church.

"So," Andrew said shyly, "we'd like to . . . buy you a new laptop . . . a MacBook, actually, if that's okay. We're ordering it tonight."

Travis and I stared at them, wordless, tears welling and overflowing from the eyes of everyone in the room. Sometimes, God makes little circles in our lives—full connections that go from joy to heartache all the way back around to a full heart once again.

Back home in Arkansas, we received our new MacBook Pro. Six years later, it is still the one I use to write on Saturday mornings, the one my boys have watched *The Magic School Bus* on, the one that holds evidence of a life held and known by God. The fire of God comes to us in moments such as these, where grief meets deep gratitude.

We grieve and then we receive, and these events don't always make sense to us in our time and in our way. But the little circles God draws in our lives, the connections from one person to another, the meeting of needs, the kindnesses that are poured out over cups of coffee and nights of thankful tears—those are the things that make up a Kingdom of glory, heaven come to earth, holy moments that give themselves to us in ordinary places, light born from darkness.

Jesus,
For all needs met,
we thank you.
For all that you've restored,
we say that we don't understand,
but we're forever grateful.
We say that you are a Mystery,
but you always know
how your mysteriousness will unfold.
And in that, we are fully
held and fully cared for.
Hallelujah,
that you are over all of it.
Amen.

28. GOATS AND CHICKENS

Is shalom kind of like Jesus? —ELIOT CURTICE, MY SON

*M*ulberry Community Garden has a small family of goats and chickens that rest and live under the shade of a big mulberry tree. We went there first with Therie, her son Noah, and little newborn Finn—the one other family we'd met in our city who was homeschooling their boys the way we were. They brought us to this little treasure they'd discovered a few months earlier, and when my boys first saw those goats and chickens, a new door opened in their hearts, and they were smitten. We promised each other that we'd come back, that we'd care for these creatures and honor their little home in the middle of our city, and we've been back numerous times since.

One night I took my boys there after dinner, after a full day of failed attempts to coax them out of wrestling with each other in our tiny apartment. We drove out to visit our creature friends, feeding them plants and fallen mulberries from their home tree. I'm not sure these animals realize what kind of magical home they inhabit next to numerous garden plots, but my two boys certainly recognize it.

In all the grandeur of this sky-scraped city, they get to spend an hour with their new friends, an hour to care for something, to spend their energy staining their fingers black with mulberry juice while I sit and watch in awe of the way the universe works.

This, for now, is all the evidence I need that things were created to work a certain way, a beautiful cycle of one creature caring for the next, that creature caring for their kin, and so on.

When a grad school semester ends for my husband, we all feel it— the pull to get away, to spend all afternoon in the kayak on the lake, to roam and journey and experience more of the world outside us.

Sometimes it is the moon's precious shape that reminds us, sometimes the glimmer of stars or the bloom of a flower.

We saw more goats at Bevin and Rowen's little commune on the other side of Atlanta. There were rabbits and sheep in a petting zoo, horses that looked you in the face and ate apples from your hand, and a giant chess board with plastic pieces that shone in the afternoon sun.

Another glimpse of Kingdom. Even there, we saw the way things are wired to work, as we fed apples to the horses, their eyes twinkling at our boys to thank them for the morning visit.

We seem to be wired for this, for the escape, for the getaway car that takes us outside of ourselves, outside of the comfort zones, outside of the closed-in spaces, to visit chickens and goats, to remember another part of life, to recognize the full cycle, and to get the full picture.

And when we return home to nap in our beds, to eat a hearty lunch, to watch a favorite cartoon, we remember that we call ourselves blessed, everything around us gift, the presence of God in our very midst, every little thing created for us to care for and have care for us.

God,

If there is some mysterious order of things that holds
    the world together,

we don't really know about it.

What we know is what we see and feel and touch,

what we partake of with the senses.

We know how to feed each other,

we take in beauty,

we share moments with created things,

to remember that we are tethered to each other

for a greater and deeper good,

for a true and lasting holiness.

This seems to be Kingdom
    as best we can understand it.

This seems to be Kingdom where Kingdom can be

understood in tiny bits and pieces,

tiny things that keep us longing for more of you.

Amen.

29. GLEN

Music expresses that which cannot be said and on which it is impossible to be silent. —Victor Hugo[38]

Last year, we were traveling to the Midwest for my husband to attend an academic conference, so we decided to spend Thanksgiving weekend with my mom and stepdad while we were there.

A month before the trip, we bought tickets for a Glen Hansard concert as the national tour pulled through St. Louis. In the early days of our love, Travis and I had listened to Glen's voice, to the Swell Season and the soundtrack to the movie *Once*. And when we moved to Atlanta, his new album serenaded me on long drives across the city and while I scrubbed dishes at my kitchen sink—my worship for this season.

On the night of the concert, we ran from the hotel room, where my parents spent the evening with the boys. I was giddy. We quickly ate dinner at a little Mediterranean restaurant across the street from the theater. We had a beer at the bar just inside the theater and waited to find our seats in the tiny auditorium.

Inside, I ate a bag of honey-roasted peanuts and drank Pepsi, and when Glen finally walked on stage, every part of our busy hearts was hushed, and we leaned forward and listened close for the voice and the instrument—

We were listening for God.

He began the show with an a cappella version of one of his songs, and I knew I'd stopped breathing by the time it was over. If I could have hushed the world, I would have, so that they could hear that still, small voice.

We tell ourselves that worship happens in the proper places at the proper times, when we go to church and do holy things and work hard to take part in the sacred and good. But it seems to me that Jesus changed that with every day that he lived, surprising people with healing by mud, with touching the untouchable, making the unholy places perfectly sacred again.

And so, we find worship where it finds us—in a small St. Louis amphitheater on a cold November night.

We lingered in the back of that little theater as long as we could until it was time to go back to the boys, and we reminded each other again that life is full and ready for living, ready for worship, ready for sacred experiences that form a deeper and deeper well within us.

I bought another album of Glen's a few months later, and I still listen to it in the mornings while I unload the dishwasher, and the Celtic storytelling that streams through his voice speaks to the Native American storyteller in me.

There are visions of hope that are asking to seep out of us if we only let them, and when they do, we experience worship. So I will keep listening to Glen's voice—he serenades me even as I write these very words.

I will keep listening to his voice because it points me back to myself and back to God, back to the gift of hope, a fire lit in the heart that cannot be put out.

Jesus,

I thank God that you knew yourself enough to be
    holy where holiness couldn't be found.

I thank God that you found yourself among the most
    broken ones, that you reminded

everything that it was good, that it was worthy, that it
    was the face of sacred love.

May we find ourselves in whatever space we inhabit,

and may we find you there where we look

and where we listen.

Hallelujah, you remain with us.

PART SIX:

Honor

ROMANS 12:9–10

Let love be genuine; hate what is evil, hold fast to what is good; love one another with mutual affection; outdo one another in showing honor.

30. HEAR ME

We are all in need of God's vision. Anything less than God's vision is broken shalom. —RANDY WOODLEY [39]

When my husband, Travis, wants our boys to really hear what he's trying to tell them, he leans down beside them and says, "Hands on my face." Eliot and Isaiah take their little palms and press them against his cheeks, and they look right into each other's eyes as if to say, *I see you, and you see me.*

When we are having a particularly hard day, it is the moment that grounds us back to each other, reminds us that we belong to each other, that the work of doing family is about loving and noticing, about listening and caring, about our hearts and our souls.

This act reminds both father and sons that all shall be well.

There is an old story about a father and his two boys. When things go badly and the youngest runs away and spends all his money, the father waits and waits for that runaway son to return home. And when things get shaken up even more, when that son finally shows up, he pulls that youngest boy to his heart.

"Hands on my face," he says. And when the oldest throws his own tantrum, when he fights for his rights, the father beckons him in, too.

"Look in my eyes," he whispers. It doesn't end all hurt or cease all tantrums, but it's the active love of seeing and hearing, of being a constant to two wavering and learning little hearts.

When I watch Travis place their hands on his face, I'm watching the holy act of reconciliation, a practice that generations of fathers and sons, lost and found, broken and more broken, have entered into out of love for one another's humanity.

And I am pulled back again, journeying back home like those sons, back into the Father's beckoning.

"Hands on my face," he says.
"Look in my eyes," he says.
And again and again until Kingdom come.

Jesus, Forever Friend,
A world of pain surrounds us—
open wounds and raised scars, shortness of breath.
Children cannot be children
   and parents lose their steps and we all
fall,
fall,
fall.
Death takes our heartbeats and flings open the
   floodgates of
"We should have" and
"I never forgave . . ."
We are paralyzed in the kneeling position, because
   nothing else makes sense
and words can't even fail because they weren't there
   in the first place.
Our grief is a blanket around us, and we cannot
   uncloak ourselves.
We mock each other's grief and lose ourselves in our
   wildernesses,
and we are undone.
Humanity beckons for you.
Lean nearer.

Lean nearer and hear with the deepest part of your
    love.
Answer us with the presence of your flesh, as tangibly
    as you can hold us
with air and space and Spirit and shalom.
We light the candles and the flames throw
    themselves in our hearts, and we sit in holy
    remembrance
of all that's been, in holy hope of all that will be.
We ache.
Relieve us, we pray.
Amen.

31. BENEDICTION

Our life comes from the very substance of God's life.
—J. Philip Newell[40]

I listened to Julie's voice on the church's blog every week. We were moving from Arkansas to Georgia in mere months, and this woman's love for her congregation was seeping through the MacBook speakers. I stood in my kitchen looking out the tiny window at Fayetteville's college-town skyline.

After we moved, Julie's words met me in person in the fellowship hall of First Baptist Church, and her presence called me back to God. When the service was over, she stepped back to the front, raised up her arms, and called out to us, called out to our callused and afraid and hoping-for-faith places:

May the God who seeks you find you when you fall.
May the God who loves you take delight in your living.
May the God who sends you send you now with joy.
For in your gladness and in your grieving;
in your brokenness and in your healing;
in your faithfulness and in your leaving,
the God who made you and redeemed you
is the God who keeps you, still.
Amen.

When I realized I'd stopped breathing to accept this message, I let out a sigh.

Yes, that's for me, I thought as I let God place me back into a space of giving and receiving with this new church. A few months later Julie stepped away from the congregation, and that next winter she moved to another state to speak life over another church. I sent her off with blessings, sent her to the next step in her journey toward God, toward wholeness and newness and life abounding, toward *glory*.

We went back to Arkansas for a few weeks that summer, back into worlds we hadn't seen for quite some time. While we were there, I saw the trajectory of our lives so far—the friends we'd left and the new friends we'd found. I saw again that in different seasons of life, God asks different things of us. In our communities, we are called into times of shaping, healing, molding, and seeking. And here, now, our church is doing all of those things—seeking and asking and trying not to be afraid when things are a little rocky and unsure.

So, we step deeper in. We ask how we can love. We seek to serve. We cherish these moments and these spaces, and we understand that God calls us, once again, into a new kind of benediction, a new kind of asking for Mystery to become concrete to us.

Julie's words have never seemed truer, and God's kindness never seemed fresher, because when we are tired, Kingdom beckons. And when we can't see what's ahead, a path is cleared, and we are no longer afraid, for glory lines the path at our feet, benedictions abounding.

Jesus,
You speak fullness over us,
forever and always.
So, move and speak.
We see you,
we're aching toward you,
hoping that your truth
really stretches and covers
all things,
everything.
We need you to be you,
and we need to find that
in all of our wandering.
Amen.

32. THE EBENEZERS

How can you seek God if he's already here? It's like standing in the ocean and crying out, "I want to get wet." You want to get over the line to God. It turns out he was always there. —DEEPAK CHOPRA[41]

When you leave a meaningful experience, or you're changed, or you see a new side of life that you weren't aware of before, it's only appropriate that you take from it an Ebenezer, a sign that God was there in your midst.

We met Mike and Cathy, a couple older than we were but also experiencing their first conference with International Justice Mission. We became instant friends, and over that short weekend we became as close as children and their parents. A few years later, they visited us when I was full-bellied pregnant, and we ate pizza and talked about the Mystery of God that pulls people to each other and deeper into a goodness that cannot be fully understood.

I went to visit Cathy and Mike one weekend in September, right before my birthday, and right before the fall equinox. In Minnesota, the air was already turning crisp and people were wearing their fall layers, preparing themselves for the coming northern winter.

We attended a conference that weekend called *Why Christian?*, the first of its kind. We heard women speak about the church, about the Jesus they knew who bled with the brokenhearted and used spit and dirt to heal. He was the Jesus who used anyone and everyone to love, to be the church, to give life to the weary.

And I realized that weekend that he was also the type of guy who might grab a rock or two as an Ebenezer, just like Cathy does. He's one who remembers, who counts the sacredness of human experience as something to be honored.

When we came back to the house from the conference, I found a pile of Ebenezers on a table right by the back porch. You only know if you stoop down and look closely that the rocks are from all over the world. Her Ebenezers. I ran my fingers over the names marked on each one, places she's visited, spaces in which she has experienced and known God.

London.

Honduras.

California.

Greece.

New Zealand.

The places are written in permanent marker on the faces of the stones. They are forever reminders of experiences, of people and places, stories of glory. Three days later, I was on a plane headed back to Georgia. The cool air was evaporating with every lift in altitude, and I knew it—I knew I needed something to hold on to, something to remind me, some piece of that holy experience. But I'd forgotten to grab a Minnesota rock. I'd forgotten before the plane was up in the air and I was untethered.

What I had was a plane ticket home and a voucher for a free drink. I ordered a Heineken, sat back with my journal and pen, and remembered. I looked at that can, that tiny tower of aluminum that reminded me of who I was just three days before the trip, and who I'd suddenly become. A few days earlier, I'd never flown by myself before. A few days earlier, I'd never gone on a trip alone with the expectation of meeting God in a new way. Now, I was seeing something new in myself. I was seeing that maybe God was doing something new inside of me, another side of Mystery that I hadn't seen before. I knew things were different, because before that moment I would have never considered buying a Heineken on a plane without a full dinner first. Instead, I had a pack of peanuts and trusted the voice of God to lead me into something new, even though I didn't understand it.

I sat back and took a lot of deep breaths and marked the air in which I was flying with my own reminder, my own Ebenezer—*here in this space I have seen and known God.*

Jesus,
I want to know you,
and I want to remember knowing you.
If I can take pieces of my life and forge them into bits
    of remembering,
things will stick, your presence will become
more real to me
every day of my life,
and every experience will be both mine
and yours.
Teach me the art of tethering.
Hallelujah and Amen.

33. THE WORLD TABLE

Good theology always protects God's total freedom, and does not demand that God follow our rules. —RICHARD ROHR[42]

essica and Alice knew how to cook, and I knew that I'd go crazy letting them do all the food preparation for us in that tiny compound where I found myself taking an afternoon nap every day, because I didn't know what I was useful for.

It was 2009, and we were in Uganda for two full months, and at every meal there was an argument. Jessica would pile extra food on my plate.

"We must fatten you up," she'd say with a smile.

One day, I mustered my courage and met them at the counter in the tiny closet of a kitchen to learn how to peel and prepare. There were shreds of fruits and vegetables everywhere, beautiful colors I'd never seen before, at least never so fresh.

Jessica taught me to cut up a pineapple, to halve and quarter and to get to the meat without wasting any of it. She laughed and clicked her tongue, shook her head at my naivety.

Travis and I had only been married a year, and it was time to get past the cooking talents I had so poorly possessed since childhood: pizza rolls and ramen noodles, soda and white-bread sandwiches.

It was time to introduce myself to the kitchen, to a world not known to my senses or met by my untrained hands. Jessica and Alice taught me to pit avocados, taught me to grate tomatoes for sauces. Jessica and Alice brought me to the table and taught me what food is for.

When we returned home from Uganda at the end of that summer, I vowed to use more fresh fruits and veggies with our meals, to eat more beans and rice, and to always grate whole tomatoes into my pasta sauce and chili.

And now, when mangoes are ripe and in season and avocados are piled on the kitchen counter, I look and see Uganda, and I smell Uganda, and I chop and grate and peel again, remembering the journey from the girl who baked pizza rolls to the woman who makes homemade graham crackers and eats herbs fresh from the soil.

I grab the old binder that holds the many recipes I received when we first married, when I didn't know the difference between a teaspoon and a tablespoon. I look through the pictures of prepared dishes, at the directions and ingredient lists, and I remember who I was when we first met.

Now, I throw basil into the food processor, grab some garlic and toss it in, too. I make pesto without the help of anything, just with the way it feels in my hands, just with the way it looks as the blade cuts it to pieces and swishes it up and onto the sides of the bowl.

I never thought I'd be here today, with my own bread in our freezer and no pizza rolls in sight. I never thought I'd be here, but the process has carved out something holy in me, in all of it.

The table is a sacred place, and everything we do to get there is also holy, including the hard work of preparation. It's sustenance, but it's also a sort of nucleus that holds us together, that calls us into its center to remember our day and remember our ties to each other.

And it all happens as food is spooned into our mouths, as we laugh and engage and embrace each other at the holy hearth of mealtime, after we give thanks for those weathered hands that prepared it, and the memory of women like Alice and Jessica who so lovingly teach others what it means to work for and honor that good sustenance.

Jesus,
I am convinced that your flesh parts loved food just
    as much as we do today.
I imagine you and your mom in the kitchen,
making flatbread and eating olives fresh from the
    yard.
I imagine your lips curling into a smile of ease,
because you knew the safety of that place, the good
and holy ground that you stood on.
Teach us to remember you,
to remember your humanity
in our own.
Even at the table,
even as we chop and sift and crack and pour,
may we see your hands guiding ours,
just as your spirit guides ours
from here to there and there to here.
Hallelujah for the establishment of mealtime,
and for the good work and the senses that lead us
    there.
Amen.

34. MIDNIGHT MEMORIES

When the grandmothers speak, the world will begin to heal.
—HOPI PROVERB

One night this last summer, I had a vivid dream about my Grandma Downing's house, the one in Ringling, Oklahoma, with a lot of farmland behind it and a shed next door where my Granddad had his own space. I dreamt about the big trees that my brother and sister climbed, about the attic and the back porch where we ran around with my Uncle Michael and Uncle Damon.

I haven't seen that house since childhood, and the bits of memories I have are wrapped up in my own heart and family photos and stories of how we played there. But I can still smell the biscuits and bacon and fried eggs, and I can still remember the way Grandma told me not to sing at the table with a stern but loving glimmer in her eye.

I dreamt that a friend of ours bought the house and remodeled it, repurposed it to fit their lifestyle today. They busted out walls and opened wide spaces wider. They invited me to see the newly remodeled space, and when I entered, I walked through the house and wept.

I wept for my father's mother, a woman that I couldn't see anymore, a woman I hadn't seen for years before she died when I was in high school. I wept because I missed her presence, her spirit, which I had felt close to as a toddler when I'd run through her yard and kitchen and play with the long strands of pearls that were hanging on her vanity mirror.

I wept because I knew that in reality the house burned down when I was in college and isn't there anymore. In reality, another house lives there and the memories of my Grandma and Granddad are buried in the dirt where the groundhogs live in the pasture.

I woke from the dream with tears in my eyes, and I couldn't let go of the memories. I spent the morning recalling, looking through that old house with my mind's eye, seeing the back porch full of wasps' nests and old furniture; the kitchen TV that played *Wheel of Fortune* religiously every evening; the side room with the giant freezer and an extra refrigerator to feed the whole family when they came to visit; the door that opened to the attic stairs, all the way up to that stuffy room where my siblings and cousins played school and read books and pretended to be ghosts; the front porch where the aloe plant stood in the corner and old china dishes sat in a hutch.

Something about that place is embedded in who I am, from the tarantula that crawled across the back of my foot to the plants and kittens we played with in the backyard.

Something from that place still invades my senses every now and then, still reminds me that Grandma Downing is there helping shape me all these years later. Her voice still brings me back to all of my ancestors, to indigenous roots that claim me, even today.

That house comes back to see me in a dream, and in its transformation I remember that I am being constantly re-created and molded and formed, constantly sent back to find who I am after all these years, and where the house will take me later in life.

God,
Dreams are the funniest things, and
when we ask for them,
you don't always answer
in the way we'd hope.
Sometimes you answer
in odd and surprising ways,
sometimes calling us back
to something that has
long been forgotten.
And the remembering
can be painful
and hard
and we may not
be willing.
But there
in the quiet of sleep
we find that your presence
leads us into and out of ourselves,
back and forth across thresholds
that we cannot control.
And as we process ourselves,
our life stories, we are thankful that
you cherish them and ask us to recall

key moments, to learn to cherish
our own lives in our own way.
Thank you for that.
Amen.

35. SECTION 10

One lives in the hope of becoming a memory.
—ANTONIO PORCHIA[43]

There's a spot at the cemetery nearby that I go to sometimes when I am alone. I lay out a quilt and rest right next to the tombstone with the name *Addy* carved in.

I'm not really sure if it's okay, if the family of *Addy* would want me laying myself down here, but I mean no disrespect. I'm here to breathe, to honor all these lives around me.

Speir, all four of them;

Grimell;

Woodward;

Robert and Julia Chandler, who both died before I was born.

This dirt-covered ground that holds their bodies knows a part of their story I don't, and so maybe if I lie still here, I'll learn a bit about my own journey.

I've been thinking a lot about the idea of labyrinths lately. A labyrinth is a walked path that teaches you to journey backward and forward to get from beginning to end. It is about process, not about a constant means to an end.

That seems the way we should be wired, but over years and years of Western thought and living, we've somehow boiled it all down to tally marks and calculations, everything walked on a straight line. A labyrinth teaches us something different.

And at this cemetery, my soul walks a labyrinth.

I begin where I am, and I walk back and forth again and again, this way and that, asking all the while what it's teaching me. I read books and watch yellow finches and hear buzzing bees doing their work, pedestrians walking through the cemetery's small roads, and I am in the journey. And these headstones around me are the Ebenezers, marking each journey, each step, each life for me to learn from.

I learn the cycle here, lessons told and retold throughout the human experience. Birds talk to each other, and trees stand tall in the knowledge of all they've seen through the years, every funeral ceremony and burial conducted under their canopies.

If I am to learn something here in this particular sanctuary, it's the cycle—that circle-of-life vision—and one day I hope a young person finds their way to my headstone to sit and pray and remember that I once had a story and that my soul walks a journey, forever circling a labyrinth of glory steps.

O God,
If you are the journey
and the journey's end,
that, of course,
means that we live on and on,
journeying forever,
back and forth,
back and forth,
finding you
and finding you again.
Hallelujah,
the journey does not stop
here
and it does not stop there,
because you,
O God,
are unending.
Amen.

36. WHERE THE HOUSE ONCE STOOD

Hold on to what is good even if it is a handful of earth.
Hold on to what you believe even if it is a tree which stands by itself.
Hold on to what you must do even if it is a long way from here.
Hold on to life even when it is easier letting go.
Hold on to my hand even when I have gone away from you.
—PUEBLO BLESSING[44]

We pulled the car up the driveway that had been shortened by the demolition of the house. Where our home used to be, there was a hole of red dirt and clay surrounded by orange plastic fencing. We sat there and remembered that three-bedroom Fayetteville home overlooking the trees of our city. It wasn't quite a weight, but a layering on of memories, a moment to stop and say *thank you* again for this gorgeous life that we've been given to live into.

When we'd first moved to Fayetteville only a few years into our marriage, we found a home just down the block that had been newly remodeled and rented to us at a cheaper rate than it should have been. We could see grace radiating from our landlady's eyes as she looked us up and down and decided that we'd be trustworthy with her rental home.

We lived there for two years, brought home our first baby boy to that living room. In the giant backyard, we watched our husky and chocolate lab run wild; we built raised beds in the corner and accumulated a heap of compost in the other corner. It was a lovely home.

After two years, we began praying about what it would mean to move out, to find something cheaper in the vicinity, and that's when Ruth from up the road knocked on our door. She said that four houses down from us there was a vacancy, and she believed we should fill it.

We worked through the process, and a few months later moved into this house down the road, right next door to Ruth and two houses over from Suzan.

Here, at this empty lot, there used to be a full house in which we ran and played, the house I brought our second boy home to, the house where we gathered with friends in community and spent mornings praying over every little thing we could imagine.

We can look back at where we once were and see something in hindsight, all the good and the bad, all the realities mingled together to give us a fuller picture of what it means to live.

We came on this trip to Fayetteville because we had a few days free. We drove eleven hours straight through, pulled into my best friend Meg's driveway, and unlocked the front door. Inside, everything welcomed us. Everything told us that we were home, that we were taken care of, that we were safe where we stood and where we rested.

We arrived quietly because we needed a trip just for us, for our rest, for our revival. We needed to remember the places that birthed us alive years ago when we lived there, spaces that speak of God's presence over us and to us still.

And when we drove through the old neighborhood, back past Ruth's house and up into Suzan's driveway, we remembered what it has meant for God to know us. We remember every time we see those flowers blooming on either side of the yard and the hammock swing on the front porch and Suzan's dog, Buster, wagging his tail and welcoming us in with his low bark.

We remember every time that God embedded a mysterious love into our life through the most unexpected women, through the most unexpected friendships.

Where that hole is, something new will be built, but that red dirt will remember us, and the people who lived there before us. That red dirt will speak of us, will speak of the way God saw us and knew us and breathed life into our empty spaces.

And when, one day, a new neighborhood is built up in those spaces where old houses once were, when generations have passed and families have filtered in and out again and again, God will still be there, presence and peace and life will still be there, and things will hold together, down to the deepest roots in the ground where dwelling places once stood.

O God,
Once a long time ago,
when there was only dirt and grass
and open spaces all over, neighbors were still
finding each other.
People were still gathering together on the grass
and spreading out their animal skins
and making plans together
under the spread of your sky.
Then one day,
we punctured that ground with
tent stakes and held our spaces together
with mud, because we needed shelter,
a way to build something together.
And later, when buildings
popped up here and there and the dirt became
stone foundations, we found ourselves
huddled on neighborhood blocks and across cities,
up and down on apartment floors.
But in all of it, we were searching for
each other, and for life with you.
We were searching the grass,
searching our floors, searching the sky,
for a sign that we were never

meant to be alone.
And indeed,
you have always given us one another.
Hallelujah and Amen.

PART SEVEN:
Worship

PSALM 63:2–4

So I have looked upon you in the sanctuary,
> **beholding your power and glory.**

Because your steadfast love is better than life,
> **my lips will praise you.**

So I will bless you as long as I live;
> **I will lift up my hands and call on your name.**

37. THE EARLY CHURCH

You think because you understand "one" you must understand "two,"
because one and one make two. But you must also understand "and."
—Sufi saying

In our early married churchgoing days, we attended a little nondenominational congregation, grace-based in belief and charismatic in worship. For community group, we spent the evenings in Justin and Kari's home with their four kids.

I'd sit in the kitchen and watch Kari do what she does—scrub the sink clean, speak to me about what it means to walk in the Spirit while making dinner for all of us and cleaning out the coffee grinder. She taught me how to eat dark chocolate and sprout raw almonds, how to drink wine and laugh.

We could hear Justin playing guitar in the living room, and worship permeated our air, blending with the smell of that ground coffee.

I learned a new language of community with these people. I learned family and meal-sharing—how to speak about being a parent without actually being one.

I just watched them most of the time, and it was a blessing to be brought into their kind reality. I didn't take it lightly. Kari showed me what the all-encompassing role of mother and wife and church leader and friend and psychologist and rock climber looks like.

It's been years since we've been with that community, in that particular home, but I can picture it still. I can see the blue and gray hues in the front room and see Uriah and Avery playing chess with Travis at the kitchen table. I can smell the brewed cup of coffee that Justin just poured and hear Rhoen screaming as he runs through the house, laughing. Cana is hanging off her dad's arms, gymnast that she's always been.

And I see our little church, hands lifted in worship, bodies swaying to the rhythm of music and Spirit.

I remember the way we prayed together, the way we sought God together, the way we screwed up together and tried our best to take grace anyway.

On Sunday mornings long before church started, I worked in the kitchen with Lissa and Bailey, the breakfast crew that would bake cinnamon rolls and rearrange messy drawers and brew the coffee for everyone to drink throughout the service.

That community was where Travis and I learned to lead small groups, with our whole selves thrown in, just like our friends Justin and Kari before us. They live in a new place now, and I try to picture their family space, the adventures they go on every day, the way they face life and work and worship as a family.

And when I scrub my kitchen sink, *every single time*, I think of Kari and that church, that community that birthed us into our marriage and carried us for a few short years before we moved on to a new season in a new town.

That early church and those early people poured life into us, helped us shape the soil we would let ourselves grow out of, letting our roots reach down past the mud to get to the water-source.

One season, years and years ago, long before us, the earliest church shaped another group of people, people who learned to care for each other and share their possessions and speak of soul-things. Maybe they ate almonds and dark chocolate and drank coffee, too.

Maybe they cultivated their soil the same way we did, tending to the roots that would one day be fruitful and grow a world that longs to know and belong to God.

Hallelujah for that early church and the many generations of community that have come after her.

Holy Spirit,
I wonder how it felt for you to blow through
that place all those years ago,
like a caged bird suddenly sweeping its wings
freely across the world outside.
You were already around,
already present,
but something new happened there
and something steady and good
took place from that day on.
You became a kind of tangible thing
that they'd always longed for
and were probably afraid to know.
But there you were,
and today you're still sweeping by,
still invading and speaking
and bringing so much
good that we could
never understand it all
with our human hearts.
Still, sweep by us
and into us
and make us
wholly yours.
Amen.

38. THE GREAT CLOUD

When we come to know our inner God, which is our true self, we will know that the divine is in everybody. —HOWARD MURPHET [45]

W ho, exactly, is in the great cloud of witnesses described again and again in the Christ-seeking tradition?

One afternoon I put the boys down for their naps and exchanged a few emotional text messages with a friend. She was about to release her first book, all nerves and excitement. And I am on the journey of writing, the journey of discovering and asking and seeking for the sake of a fuller human experience.

So, from my little apartment living room, thinking of my friend sitting in her living room, I pictured her there, resting at the edge of a vast ocean.

Instead of walls, there were waves.

Instead of household sounds, there was only the full crash of water crest upon water crest—with the sight of leaping fish and reflected sunlight against blue salt.

We're both overcome by the goodness of God. We're both seen, known, held, just like Moses and Saul-turned-Paul, just like Mary Magdalene and Hagar.

The great cloud of witnesses is you, and it is me.

It is the way we surround each other, the way we share seasons and dreams. It is in the quiet of our living room as we stare into those depths, as we sense the kind hands that sweep over all of it.

It is the woman at the grocery store who flirts with my boys and says, "I remember those days. Cherish them." It is the pedestrian crossing the street at the corner of Church and Ponce. It is my barista, Katherine. It is Blaze, Rozie, Mishma, Chavez, Shaq, and Chance, the servers who have become family at a local burger restaurant we eat at every Sunday.

The great cloud is made up of the ones gathered around us, people whose pulse marks the breath of God, whose very being shows evidence of what is sacred.

It is the gay man to my right and the straight man to my left, the conservative and the progressive, both pumping the same gasoline.

We make up the witnesses, the people who can criticize the church and still love her deeply, because we claim the Resurrection. We claim these days of glory, these moments of reconciliation and presence, of grace and Kingdom.

We ask God if the Kingdom is even there, all the while trusting it to be closer than ever.

We are the great cloud.

We are the ones who see God,

the ones who are seen by Mystery.

Hallelujah for that kind of glory.

O God,
If we make it to our old and gray days,
    show us who we were all those years before.
When we are welcomed into your eternal fold,
    let us look back with you—
into all the dark places, into all the light.
So that we see what you see,
know what you know
and understand
that you held us all those years,
in all those seasons,
right there in the midst
of our everyday breathing.
Hallelujah
and Amen.

39. A CHURCH FOR THE CHILDREN

Occasionally it is not the open air or the church that we desire, but both.
—J. Philip Newell [46]

For our first two years in Georgia, every time we drove Travis to campus, we'd pass an abandoned church a few miles from our apartment complex, and Eliot would ask why it was abandoned and what would happen to the empty building. Those questions came after he commented on how beautiful it was.

After being away for two weeks last summer, we came home to find demolition of that church building had begun. The next weekend, the bell tower had finally fallen, all was dirt and twisted metal, the bell nowhere to be seen.

"Mommy, will our church be ripped down one day like that one?" Eliot asked.

Our children ask the really difficult questions, the ones we're afraid to whisper to the outside air; they are brave.

And I replied, "Oh, sweetie, I hope not, but we don't really know."

Today, the children are asking what the church is, how she is strong and good, and what she will look like in the years ahead. Even after being in Georgia for barely a year, Eliot and Isaiah had already noticed the denominational divides. They know the Methodists' bell tower from the Baptists' columns, the Presbyterians' steeple from the Episcopalians' color-tinted windows.

Eliot sees church as building—stone, brick, paint, rooms—and we must remind him that church is Kingdom, too—people, nature, life abounding.

Church is Thursday afternoons with Leanna. Church is sheep-watching with Joss and Debra. Church is eating the home-grown veggies Hannah gifted to us. Church is an evening at the climbing gym with Daniel and Connor and the boys' favorite staff member, Shawn.

Church is the farmers market on the lawn. Church is the international market where we buy our groceries. Church is Taproom coffee where I read Richard Rohr and drink my latte.

Church is the holy and good encouragement of a weekly gathering with people we dearly love and fight for. Church is *us*—you, me, our aunts and uncles and children and neighbors, and sometimes our enemies, too.

The Kingdom is not bound by brick walls, not hemmed in by any denomination's guidelines. It doesn't exist only when the bells are tolling the church hour.

So when our children see churches fall, we remind them of the good gifts given, of the body and the blood, of the faces and names and stories that make up the heart of God here on earth.

And maybe then we ourselves will learn from our little ones' glorious light to become brave. They teach us to stand taller with one another, to kneel lower to be with God, and to boldly ask for more Kingdom, even in our darkest hours.

A friend asked me what I'd like the church to look like for my boys ten years from now.

"I want them to ask the same childlike questions that they are asking now—and I want the church not to be afraid to ask them those same questions," I said after a long pause.

Our children see the things we do not see, understand Jesus in ways we have long forgotten. They hold the capacity to redefine the church, to reawaken hearts. If we teach our children that church is Kingdom and Kingdom is church in our everyday breathing, in everyday glory, then she will never die—horizons will be forever open on every side.

Oh, Jesus, may we think outside again.
May we look to the rest of the world,
to the "other,"
to the broken,
not to fix them,
but to receive from them,
to share in life with them.
Jesus, you gave everything you were to all of us,
but you also let us become a part of you.
So help us learn to be a part of each other.
We're in so much need.
Amen.

40. INVEST

It is your birthright to experiment and dare and pioneer as if the sole boundary holding you is the love you are guided by.
—ERIKA MORRISON [47]

*I*t is the second time we've come together for contemplation in the six-week Lenten study at First Baptist Church. We gather into our circle of chairs, facing each other, all six of us huddling closer than we think comfortable, but close enough to do the necessary work of communal quiet.

I've never taught a class outside the comfort of my kitchen table and living room floor, where the rules are very easy and things flow just as they need to.

Here, we are in stiff chairs; there is no meal, no warmth of bookshelves and couches, candles and family, but we are ready and willing to find ourselves and each other anyway.

We ask together what it means to give something up, to look deeper, to ask who we're supposed to be in the quiet when no one else is listening but our heart and God's ears.

I pass out index cards, each one filled with a word written in royal-blue permanent marker ink:

Trust.

Peace.

Dream.

Gifts.

And on mine, *Invest.*

I start the timer on my phone, ten minutes to sit and think and pray and try to be quiet enough to hear something of God, even if it's the stillness of his breathing over us.

I ask myself what it means to invest in something; I want so badly to grab my iPhone and look up the definition, so it can be really clear for me.

But I wait.

I decide on my own synonyms, my own understandings.

To invest in something means that I give energy to it.

I give sweat to it.

I live in it and move in it.

It means that I'm trying to shape something, but that I'm letting something shape me, I write.

I wait a little longer, because the problem with blank pages is that I write and write and never notice God's breath at all.

So I keep praying.

You've always invested in me.

You poured your energy out.

Every healing required part of your Spirit, until the day you finally spilled your own sweat and your own blood, so I could know you here, in this place.

You've invested in me, I write.

And then he pours out breath, gives me words and kindnesses and the reminder of his presence.

Keep going, he says.

Keep sharing.

Keep giving,

keep writing,

keep believing,

keep trusting in my presence

and its life to your daily dying bones.

If ever one invested in another, Jesus has invested in me. He's been the friend, the comforter, the only hope, the provider, the gift-giver.

And every time, glory comes all over again as a fresh wave, a new revelation, a secret long kept, which has burst from the lips of God, and I am redeemed in that quiet ten minutes of contemplation.

When we are all in that circle, looking at each other's faces, watching each other's hands fidget with discomfort, we understand the holy things that happen in community, in sitting and being with one another, even when it's unbearably silent.

There, we understand that the carpet beneath us is like the ground Moses stood on, the ground that God called holy when he asked for faith and trust in the quiet of the hills and beside the burning of the bush.

Jesus,
Teach us to redefine our world.
May we redefine all the words we once used
for our own benefit,
and may forgiveness not be for the heathen,
but for our own tired selves.
May lament, joy, honesty, and compassion lead us
toward investing in the love you first started
when you breathed your first breath.
You teach us what it means
to redefine our world.
Amen.

41. THE ROCKS

We need the tonic of wilderness—to wade sometimes in marshes where the bittern and meadow-hen lurk, and hear the booming of the snipe. . . . At the same time that we are earnest to explore and learn all things, we require that all things be mysterious and unexplorable, that land and sea be infinitely wild, unsurveyed and unfathomed by us because unfathomable. We can never have enough of Nature.
—HENRY DAVID THOREAU [48]

he first time I saw my husband, Travis, rock climb, we'd been together for a few weeks, and didn't quite grasp that we'd be married seven months later. He wore these thin, tan-colored hemp pants, and when he slipped on his yellow climbing shoes, I knew something holy was happening.

I'd never played sports in school, because track, basketball, volleyball, or soccer never interested me enough to try. I wasn't competitive with other people or motivated enough to give my time away.

I'd never really heard of rock climbing, not the kind that brought this spark of glorious being to the man I quickly grew to love. It was a kind of communion: Travis engaging the realities of God with a rope and harness as he climbed the side of a cliff.

But after watching him, I began to notice rock faces and outdoor marvels like I never had before.

I saw this new kind of adventuring, this beautiful sport that was more extreme than anything I'd experienced, a more artistic and natural, all-encompassing lifestyle that was fully awake to the outside world-wilderness.

Shortly after we were married, we went camping at Horseshoe Canyon Ranch, and it was the first time in years that I'd camped with anyone. It was also the first time my young, conservative Christian nose had ever smelled pot as a group of strangers lit their joints outside our tent door.

153

I'd brought a small DVD player so we could watch a movie in the tent that evening. Because I was uncomfortable with this environment, I completely missed the opportunity to embrace my husband's love of the natural world and this community of kind and wild people who called it home.

We spent some time climbing the next day, and that tiny spark was being lit slowly in me, a sliver of the love I'd one day feel for the rock faces and the shining sun.

After we had kids, we climbed less and less because it was hard to know how to find the time. But I always saw that longing in his eyes, and quietly prayed for the day he would get his climbing shoes and harness out from under the bed and begin again. Every spring, it seems, or at the end of a momentous season, Travis pulls up some climbing videos on YouTube and shows the boys this world that he adores and longs to return to.

Last spring he climbed for the first time in years, and his muscles quickly remembered their old ways, his body and soul aching to be outside against the rocks again. We joined a climbing gym in the city as a family; Travis and I watched the boys shimmy up a wall as high as we are tall. With our own climbing, we felt muscles coming alive, with body aches as the result of new movement and healthy habits.

There's a shift that happens to our life passions when we get married and have kids, and sometimes we protect those passions, and other times we let them go.

But when I see my husband and boys watch videos of Chris Sharma climbing a rock face in France, I can see it—a future of father and sons trekking outdoors for kayaking, hiking a secret trail, bouldering around the wilderness.

One adventure leads to another, and they find themselves in the fire of their passions, their mother watching them as she trails along close behind, praying for the opportunity to be let into that holy space.

O God,
When you created the rock faces,
did you see the places
we'd all climb one day,
the little crevices that would
bring such unexpected
challenge and joy to the people
who try to climb them?
Surely you knew we'd
find ourselves there,
find our souls
and our spirits
come to life
in the glimmering sun
against the hot stone structures,
inside the face of the bonfire.
I believe you knew it all,
great Mystery that you are,
and that you called it good—
the rocks and us,
the water and the waves,
the flowers and the fields,
all creation coming together for an
uncommon reunion,

for a holy communion
in your good, good presence.
May we always commune,
always seek you
where we know you'll be found,
until our last earthbound days.
Amen.

42. MURCHISON FALLS

All I can do is say, Here's how it went. Here's what I saw. I've been there and am going back. Make of it what you will. —LEIF ENGER, *PEACE LIKE A RIVER* [49]

While staying in Uganda for our one-year anniversary, Travis and I joined a fishing trip on the Nile River. Our friend Allan summoned us early in the morning, and so we grabbed to-go boxes of breakfast food and met our friend Doc outside by the boat.

As if seeing every animal I'd dreamt of seeing outside a zoo wasn't enough, I was captivated by watching the natural current of this famous river, the way the ripples and foam kept us moving past the hippo mothers' faces and open mouths. I was on a boat of men preparing to fish, and while I had no desire to hold a fishing pole, I had every desire to watch and be present to this experience.

I didn't want the moments on that river to pass me by without notice. I sat as still as I could; I watched Travis looking on this place he'd spent months exploring a few years earlier, this country that was a second home to him. He knew the waters and understood what the rolling hills had to say. We celebrated by that river in a hotel with a beautiful linen canopy over the bed and staff that greeted us at the door with mango juice and face wipes. It was the most pampering we'd ever received.

Years later, to celebrate our eighth anniversary, Travis bought me a vintage map of the Nile, printed in light green, yellow, and brown, and we went to see the Atlanta Symphony play with singer-songwriter Gregory Alan Isakov. As we listened, I closed my eyes. I could hear things I'd only heard before in movie soundtracks—the flittering of violin notes, melodic and free, movements that swept my heart away and begged me to awaken from every sleepy depth I found myself in.

I opened my eyes and saw the ceiling open up to a blue and gray sky, the walls fall back to reveal wide open plains. I don't know what others were imagining—every eye was entranced, unwilling to miss a moment, and every breath in the room was hushed; cups of wine came to mouths one quiet sip at a time. We were lost in this womb of magic, and I could understand why a baby, before being born, appreciates hearing voices and rhythms outside the walls of their mother's belly.

And so that night, the music of the symphony—with the banjo and the violin and the bass, the drum and the guitar and the short flight of the harp—gave husband and wife permission to remember the Nile, to see wide open spaces, to fall into each other again, seven years and two kids after that first Nile-side anniversary celebration.

One day we might make it back to the Nile, but in the meantime, we will see that map, hanging framed on the wall of our home, and we will smell mangos and buy black beans and rice and know that what once took us to that river boat might take us there again, whether in body or in spirit, in reality or in dreams.

O God,
You are the God of remembering.
You give us memories to keep,
  and you usher us in and out
of those spaces in our hearts and minds.
You remind us of who we once were,
who we are, and you challenge us to
become someone new in the days ahead.
For this, we are forever grateful,
because you never let us go,
and you never stop honoring
who we are in the in-between times.
And with every experience we see your influence,
  and so
we understand that you are not just
a bystander, but an active and good
presence in our lives, ushering us deeper
into ourselves and into you.
Deeper, deeper, and on into the sweetest of living.
Thank you for that.
Amen.

43. AUTUMN BRUNCH

We are as hungry and needy as newborn babies. We fool ourselves if we imagine anything else to be true. —CHRISTIE PURIFOY[50]

Our Sunday school class came over for brunch near the beginning of fall, right around my birthday. I set out piles of food on our tiny oak table, and I used every orange and red and yellow dish I could find to create an experience reflecting the transformation happening outside our windows.

Community at this church looks different than past churches we've been a part of, because it's a traditional model based on Sunday school every week and Wednesday night Bible study. It's the model in which I grew up, but it took us a while to understand this new dynamic for our own family.

After some time, I realized I ached to gather my friends in *my home*, to feed them and watch them examine my space, my decorating style, my book choices, to choose which chair suited them the best, to dream for themselves what it might mean to have a balcony garden. The home is a space for growth—a communal gathering place where we find ourselves and find each other—God in our midst.

That Saturday morning, I watched everyone gather in. I watched the food pile up on the plates, saw where everyone decided to sit, noticed conversations between close friends and people who barely knew each other. I saw something that doesn't happen on Sunday mornings during our hour-long class time, something organic taking shape, just what I'd prayed I would see.

When we open up our own spaces and gather people to our hearths, ask others to join us in our living, we find each other—we find God. We find fresh opportunities to dream and vision-cast; we find revived belief that the church and the people in it can be more than we've ever known.

When we sit across from each other with food piled on our plates, with hot chocolate steaming from thrift-store mugs, worship takes place. New friendships emerge that before were only tiny seeds of hope—when hands and feet and arms reach across for a hug after those few hours are over.

Everything comes into focus and bloom, and we remember why we gather together. We remember what it means to belong to each other, now and forevermore. All over a simple early fall brunch.

Jesus,
In the specks of light that hover
in your presence,
something pulls us all together.
In the specks of light that give hope
to our spaces
and remind us that we
are loved,
we see your face
in the face of our friends.
We see your breath
in our breath,
your face
in each other's faces,
feel your calloused
hands in the hands
of every encounter.
And so,
in some never-understood way,
we invade your space
and you invade ours,
a Venn diagram
where we are
enclosed in all that you are,
and you are in all of us as well.
Hallelujah and Amen.

PART EIGHT:

Kingdom

HEBREWS 12:28-29

Therefore, since we are receiving a kingdom that cannot be shaken,
let us give thanks, by which we offer to God an acceptable worship
with reverence and awe; for indeed our God is a consuming fire.

44. A DEEP NEED

The clear proof of a person's love of God is if that person genuinely shows love to fellow human beings. —TENZIN GYATSO, THE 14TH DALAI LAMA[51]

Many times, we forget that we need others. And then someone pours themselves out for us, brings us that much-needed cup of coffee, watches our kids so we can breathe a little, reminds us that we're safe and held.

When I was pregnant with Isaiah, Eliot was one year old and growing by the minute. Most days I was confined to the couch, fighting severe nausea. Most days I was clinging to the presence of Jesus in ways I never had before. Most days I was lonely and tired and longing for those nine months to pass by quickly and with less pain.

It was the worst my pregnancy had gotten, and our house was a mess, and I was sinking deeper into it. I couldn't see outside of myself, and that was the hardest part of all.

When I am not allowed to do what I need to do—to serve others and be an active part of the community—I all but fall apart. So, I sent an e-mail to my closest friends, the people who would gather in our home weekly to be human with us, to be broken with us, and to heal with us.

I told them that our house was a war zone of toys and clothes and dishes. I told them that I needed someone to help me scrub the kitchen floor. I told them that I'd feed them pizza and give them hugs as best I could.

They swarmed in, and while others cleaned up indoors, Chris and Connor tackled the outside. I hadn't realized how much dog poop was in the backyard, how many leaves were spread around, never raked in the year we'd lived there. But they cleaned it all without complaint.

A few hours later when it was over, I looked around and took mental pictures of the place—the bare floor, the organized bookshelves, the cleaned-up yard, my happy little boy. None of these people had children yet, and only a few were married. But they knew servanthood, and they knew it in a stage of life totally foreign to them.

They knew that modern-day foot-washing rituals include scrubbing laminate floors and putting dishes back where they belong. They knew my need and rescued me out of my despair—my friends as the very hands and heart of God. And I knew then that it wasn't just my needs being met, but the needs of the Kingdom, people stretching arms out to people, deeds of glory coming alive in human hearts.

I remember that morning on the couch, but today's needs look different. They are still being met, though, when Hannah comes over with fresh fruit to make smoothies, and homemade hummus, when she brings craft supplies for my boys, and when she listens as I talk about mothering. She sips coffee with me and tells me that my home is good, that my marriage is good, that I have everything I could possibly need.

So in the midst of community, everything comes full circle; the needy find refreshment and the tired find rest. And I don't think this good Kingdom would have it any other way.

O God of Mystery,
If I have tried to place you into a box,
break it.
No mold can hold you.
I search the surface of the earth
to understand you,
because we are your imprint.
But I cannot understand.
Only the kind glimpses
you give me can suffice.
And indeed, they are everything I'll need.
Teach me to look out to your bigness,
to fall freely into your Holy Abyss,
into your depths,
where I see more glimpses of Kingdom things.
It's safe and good there,
and it is where we long to be.
Bring us to you,
the One who is
not here or there,
not this or that.
We do not even understand
how we long for you,
how we burn in our bones
for your presence.
It is simply our need.
Pull us closer, still.
Amen.

45. SANCTUARY

Through daily rituals of presence, communication, and faith, we have the power to stay connected to what matters in a culture that often leads us astray. —RACHEL MACY STAFFORD[52]

Across the street from Meg's house there is a sanctuary. It is a place of safety—a red brick house with an A-line roof. In the front yard is a garden full of carrots and coneflowers, plants of many kinds.

There's an electric fence to protect them from curious predators. Nonetheless, it is a place of peace, and everything about it whispers to the stranger that the inhabitants—the creatures rooted within its borders—are cared for. And there is, within that sanctuary, a safe space for birds, numerous feeders under an archway, where they are free to be what they are.

For years, we've held services in church sanctuaries, large rooms with pews and pulpits and baptistery waters that keep us safe from the outside world. But over time, it seems, these holy places have become rooms in which fear is taught and the light that once comforted has become some sort of interrogation lamp. We are made to feel shame for all the things we've done or left undone, for all the things we think we are meant to be.

And so, sanctuary becomes Meg's front yard again, the home of a dear friend where my family can rest and be and breathe easy.

As with every trip, I bring as my companion a novel from Jan Karon's *Mitford* series, a world that comforts and walks with me through every season of my life. Her words in *Out to Canaan* offer their usual comfort and sanctuary:

The morning mist rose from the warm ground and trailed across the garden like a vapor from the moors. Under the transparent wash of gray lay the grand emerald of new-mown grass, and the unfurled leaves of the hosta. Over there, in the bed of exuberant astilbe, crept new tendrils of the strawberry plants whose blossoms glowed in the mist like pink fires.[53]

For those few days that our family stays at Meg's house on vacation, we feel it—we know those walls hold us intact, keep us tethered to each other, to community, to Kingdom and Creation.

We know that sanctuary can be an assortment of things, but that it always holds steady to what it needs to be: the resting place, the breathing place, the place that calls us safe and home.

Jesus,
You, of course, are our resting place.
But how wonderful that we have a universe
of opportunities to find solace,
to find peace,
to find that space that brings us back to ourselves
  and to you.
And where we may find it is always a surprise,
always an amazing realization
that you actually linger in this world you created
and care for,
that you are found where those
sanctuaries are found,
among the flowers,
sometimes in the church pews,
outside in nature's pathways,
inside by the fire.
Everywhere
you are solace,
and everywhere we have a chance
to find our rest and our peace.
Hallelujah,
you have provided.
Amen.

46. PRETEND PLANES

You are full of unshaped dreams . . .
You are laden with beginnings . . .
—LOLA RIDGE[54]

Travis and I gathered around a small table at a coffee shop just off the downtown square in our little college town. Eliot was strapped into his stroller next to us. It was our fourth anniversary.

The farmers market was in full bloom under the June sun right outside the door, bodies swishing to and fro with fresh fruits and veggies in their baskets, bought straight from the people who'd pulled them fresh from the ground.

We drank our latte and cappuccino, and looked ahead like we were about to celebrate the New Year and toast each other: *we'd made it, four years.*

I brought along my tiny journal, the one with scribbled thoughts that I wanted to keep. We dreamt of what we wanted for our family, for the entirety of our marriage, for the days ahead.

And I decided then and there that what I really wanted for us was the chance to see the world, to marvel at it, to take in all the mountaintops and muddied valleys, all languages, every sight and smell.

We'd started out years ago with that same dream. After two months in Uganda in 2009 on a research grant, we'd found we wanted more of the world, more cultures, more glory in more spaces. Something had been poured out, and we could not stop there.

We thirst for more air, for the smell and taste and touch of things we've never known but have always needed. That day I wrote down the new dreams: to take our boys across the oceans; to understand diversity in a new light; to simply have the means to know the world created with such vast Mystery and abundance.

I prayed for those things in the tiny place of my heart that begs to be heard.

If I find glory here, in my familiar spaces, what glory awaits me across oceans, over mountaintops, beneath a tiny pebble on a sanded beach?

And we still dream in every new season of our life together. After five years of marriage, and again now after eight, our dreams shift a little, take on new shapes, but still hold to the same heart.

I drive in the car and I pray to see more of those clouds, to watch the face of the moon from another country, to expand and expand and expand our love of people and culture and life. We still long for views of oceans, to see dolphin fins flutter and flap in and out of salty water.

We still search for mountains in our minds, hoping one day to touch their rocky surfaces. And we still cry at the color and culture promised by the world outside our door. We hold on to the dream, with two little boys at our sides and maps plastered to the walls of our tiny apartment.

And when we pretend we are airplanes, we fly from continent to continent, and Eliot screams, "It's too far!" and we rejoice.

Because that's exactly what makes the world so beautiful and so complete for our dreaming hearts, the possibility that one day we will make it to those places that seem so far out of our reach, so beyond our known experiences.

Our dreaming, our will, meshes with God's, and we learn to trust deeper and hope the way our children hope—arms spread wide, imaginations untethered.

Jesus,
I simply want your will.
I simply want who you are,
and all that encompasses you.
I do not long for more words,
but more presence.
I long for quiet from loud,
for dreams when my heart wants to see
how good you are.
I long to remember that
whatever I do or don't do,
it doesn't sway you this way or that.
Because Jesus, you're you,
all-encompassing goodness and grace,
our greatest dream-caster
and provider.
Amen.

47. THE FOUNTAIN

Catch it if you can. The present is an invisible electron; its lightning path traced faintly on a blackened screen is fleet, and fleeing, and gone.
—ANNIE DILLARD[55]

At the feet of the skyscrapers in my city, there's a large park. And if you walk far enough into that park, there's a giant circle of cement with water jets in the ground. The jets shoot fountains up into the sky, iridescent streams of water reaching up and returning in an arc to the hot ground that birthed them. There is a path all around it where children can ride their bikes, a big patch of green for picnics and Frisbee throwing.

When people are around, it's never quiet there. The air fills with laughing shrieks, teenage girls dancing with their two-year-old cousins, all splashing with eyes closed. And we see our boys come alive.

Eliot, with every extroverted corner of his soul, is electrified by these stranger-friends' smiles, by the glory-joy around him. Isaiah eases in slowly, but once the cool water touches his feet, he fights at those jets of cold with an imaginary sword, slaying the water-dragons around him.

I slice another piece of cucumber and open a cheese stick for the boys and watch them dance. Everyone stands at their own jets, but eventually they all end up back in the center, where the biggest jet sits underground. It seems to have millions of jets all in one spot, and for a moment all is quiet as the anticipation builds. Then a giant burst of water shoots up and out and all around, filling every space, soaking every part of those laughing children's bodies to the core.

It's like the hearth of the home where all gather in, where comfort and joy and fullness are found. It's the epicenter and the life source.

Sometimes it feels as if humanity is slipping away from us, that we've lost sight of each other and ourselves, that we've forgotten how to care, how to be alive, how to play and enjoy each other's company.

But then we come to the fountain. We see heaven communing on earth, in the heat of day at the stone splash pad in the middle of Piedmont Park.

These are the kinds of places made for the celebration of humanity, places that level the playing field and call us all children, call us all into the summertime baptism, where those laughing voices become the holy sounds of angels gathered at a throne of pure and benevolent grace.

Holy Fountain,
You're the thing we need.
When we are thirsty, you are our drink.
When we need to be clean, you are our bath.
When we are broken, you are our healing.
You seem to be everything to us,
and if we're lucky enough to discover your fresh life,
we find joy abounding.
We find laughter and freedom and pleasure,
green grass and Frisbee throwing and snacks
and community.
We find heaven and earth in a holy collision,
and we prostrate ourselves and say, "Finally, finally,
  Kingdom."
Amen.

48. RAPTURE

For this perishable body must put on the imperishable, and this mortal body must put on immortality. —1 Corinthians 15:53 (ESV)

*W*hen I was little, I'd always hoped that Jesus would come back while I was doing something holy, like reading my Bible or leading worship. But now I realize that he will probably come for me while I'm watching *Longmire* or *Gilmore Girls*, while I'm doing the dishes or buying groceries, while I'm reading Jan Karon and breastfeeding my newborn.

Maybe he will show up at the coffee shop where I write every Saturday, as I take my last sip of vanilla latte.

When I was little I thought God saw me most fully when my nose was in the Bible, with my sins written out in confession on a journal page. I've always wanted to be good. And I thought anything less than perfectly holy was unacceptable, that God would put a hand up and say, "That's it. One day off the track, we're through."

The wonderful thing about time never stopping and God always moving is that we get to experience Mystery and love anew every day.

We are called forgiven.

That forgiving presence is my salvation in any of those moments, and I have no need to be afraid.

When Travis and I were in Uganda, I sat with my Bible open one day, and I cried. I let my heart break over the lies I'd held onto since childhood, the image of God I'd set up as this mean judge with a gavel who sends anyone who has even a bit of a hateful bone in their body straight to the fire.

But then I walked outside and stood next to the outdoor kitchen in the Kampala compound where we were staying. I watched my husband read a book and write in his journal; I saw school children pass by and wave at me, their white teeth flashing in the afternoon sun. And I remembered God then, the One who called me good and beckoned me into a new presence, the judge who judges out of love, who calls to the broken and lives in humanity because creation is called good.

That's the rapturing God, the One who will come again and claim things, the One who may just sit down next to me and say, "Did you see that episode of *Longmire* last week?" And I'll laugh and we'll be exactly who we are with each other, dreaming for a new earth and a new life to come, resting in all the spaces in between.

Jesus,
Because you were brought forth from Mary's belly,
God saw humanity from your eyes.
Your every move was an experience of Mystery,
salvation walking on feet and reaching with hands.
Your every move made the wholeness of creation a
   reality.
And one day a new beginning will come again,
and all will know your goodness,
all will see you in a new light, in a new glory,
in a new whispering of Hallelujah
from the heights to the depths.
And something of the whole
picture will be revealed,
from all these little puzzle pieces we've been
contriving to match what we want for
our eternity.
And we rest, because you hold it all.
Amen.

49. HIJAB

"There are all kinds of courage," said Dumbledore, smiling.
—J. K. ROWLING[56]

One day while shopping at our favorite international farmers market, Eliot grabbed my hand and led me to the chocolate and candy aisle where a woman wearing a hijab stood, expecting me.

"She wants to give you one!" shouted Eliot as he pointed to her purple head covering.

Because he'd told her how beautiful she was, she offered a most beautiful gift to his mother, whom she'd just met. She told me to come back for my very own hijab the next week. On a Wednesday afternoon, I stopped by the market for fresh salmon and asparagus and there she was—stocking the shelves with chocolates.

We did not know each other's names, only faces. I apologized for not coming sooner, and she led me to the back of the store. She had been keeping two hijabs in her locker waiting for me.

"We cannot tell the managers. We cannot give gifts to customers, you see?" she said with a twinkle in her eye and a smile. She told me discreetly to wait by the assorted rice, and came back a moment later with a small gray plastic bag.

"You choose. Purple or blue with this bracelet."

I looked up at her shining face and said I'd love the blue one. We embraced, and she sent love to my little one who first introduced us through his aesthetic eye—his gift for finding beauty in the smallest and unexpected ways.

Before I drove home, I took it out of the bag and put it over my pulled-up hair and bangle earrings. I put it on and wondered what discrimination a hijab-wearing woman might endure in our culture.

I looked at the cars next to me at the stoplight and wondered what they thought, if anything. And I looked at myself in the mirror and saw how different my face was with this beautiful veil of blue around my neck and hair.

But more than that, I wondered at the God-given kindness of this elderly woman to gift me a hijab and send me off as her new friend, some sort of invisible goodness tethering us to each other and to the Kingdom of God through the beauty-loving eye of my four-year-old son.

We wonder so much about God, about humanity, about whether our everyday experiences mean something. What matters and what is dust in the wind? Do our little moments of joy or pleasure, our pings of grief and stress, mean anything on the Kingdom level?

Absolutely. Our moments matter because our humanity matters, and if we can't find it in the chocolate aisle or by the assorted rice in the middle of our local marketplace, we will have a hard time finding it anywhere.

O God,
In these corners of our lives, speak.
These days, govern and pour
out the gift of your truth
over our daily lives,
so that when this
is over and done with,
we are still there with you,
still surrounded by Christ-grace
and Spirit-breath
and God-provision.
Hallelujah, for where we are now
and where we'll be tomorrow.
Amen.

50. IN THE MEANTIME

"It is not for you to know times or seasons that the Father has fixed by his own authority. But you will receive power when the Holy Spirit has come upon you." —ACTS 1:7–8 (ESV)

Every now and then, Travis and I take a look over our life. We sit down and we remind ourselves of the way God has provided, of spiritual moments that have kept us going these past years.

Just before we moved to Georgia, we completed one of those lists—a few pages full of kindnesses that we couldn't understand, that we'd never even try to. We've been in Georgia two years now, and a few weeks ago I found that list. I ran my fingers over every word on that timeline, saw the stretch from there to here, from one season to the next. It showed me that every moment was cared for, crafted for something good and holy, something to give us meaning, something to lead us on.

All we know is that God provides, and that we are always given what we need.

There are *meantime* things that we can't worry about—Kingdom things that are so outside of us that we couldn't dare try to fathom them.

What we know is Spirit-truth, that the Spirit holds us, guides us, moves us through life.

And in that we are secure.

These *meantime* seasons remind us that what we don't understand is exactly what the Mystery of God is meant to be for us. A friend gifts us a brand new computer; someone buys me a cup of coffee; our friends babysit the boys so we can go on a date.

We are human, and we are tiny, and yet, God stretches love into us and over us and around us, and our lives become bigger, our voices stronger, our gifts more magical with each passing day that we trust in the sacredness of our life.

In the *meantime,* we wait for Kingdom things to happen.

In the *meantime,* we trust the gifts given.

In the *meantime,* we rest in community—we rest in the promise that we are not alone when God is alive and well.

In the *meantime,* we keep these memories close to our hearts, so that when Kingdom does finally come, we know exactly what to say *thank you* for.

Mystery of everything that we understand
and most certainly everything that we don't,
teach us to rest in this unknowing.
Teach us to rest in each other,
to rest in the presence of a stranger,
in the kindness that is always unexpected,
that surprises us,
that gives us a taste of you,
as much as we can bare to understand.
You are the Creation,
you are the Light,
you are the Weight,
you are the Voice.
You hold Fire,
you give Honor,
you gift Worship,
and you are Kingdom,
yesterday,
today,
tomorrow.
Hallelujah,
for all the glory.
Amen.

ACKNOWLEDGMENTS

The gratitude I've felt throughout this process has been overwhelming.

Migwetch, Mamogosnan—Thank you, Creator—I cannot say that you are not good. Your gracious presence in my human experience is everything to me.

To Travis, who spent hours with the boys so I could write at my favorite coffee shop, and who has always reminded me to trust my own voice on this journey—thank you.

To my mama, an independent woman who has taught me my whole life to think for myself and love people.

To my family, who speaks encouragement to me from a distance daily.

To my Grandma and Grandmother—your spirits helped bring these stories to life. I honor your lives in all of them.

To my church, who through their support taught me to find my voice and has never stopped supporting me since.

To Julie Pennington-Russell, for being the first person to make me introduce myself to people as a "writer."

To my editor Phil and the staff at Paraclete Press, for taking a chance on an unknown author.

To Meg, you support me in everything that I am and ever hope to be. You daily teach me grace and a kind of love that is truly, truly Kingdom. Thank you for being my best friend.

To Brian McLaren, who has supported my work and been a great advocate this last year.

To Ashley, Hannah, and Leanna, the women who have walked with me these past few years and reminded me that God is truly in my everyday living.

To Rachel Macy Stafford, for being such a dear friend and encouragement to me on my writing journey.

To Amy Paulson, for gifting me a photo session that captured my soul so perfectly and gave me the photo for this book.

To the friends who find their names and stories in this book— thank you for your presence in my life.

And to a world full of writers whose books grace our shelves and our community bookstores, your words inspire me now, and they always will.

RECOMMENDED READING

Alcott, Louisa May. *Little Men: Life at Plumfield with Jo's Boys.* Boston: Roberts Brothers, 1871.

Brooks, Geraldine. *Caleb's Crossing.* New York: Penguin Books, 2012.

Dillard, Annie. *Pilgrim at Tinker Creek.* New York: Harper Perennial, 1974.

Enger, Lief. *Peace Like a River.* New York: Grove Press, 2001.

Foster, Richard. *Celebration of Discipline, 20th Anniversary Edition.* San Francisco: HarperSanFrancisco, 2002.

Haines, Amber. *Wild in the Hollow.* Grand Rapids, MI: Revell, 2015.

Lamott, Anne. *Help, Thanks, Wow.* New York: Riverhead Books, 2012.

Levine, Steven. In *For the Love of God: Handbook for the Spirit,* edited by Benjamin Shield and Richard Carlson. Novato, CA: New World Library, 1997.

Manning, Brennan. *Abba's Child: The Cry of the Heart for Intimate Belonging.* Colorado Springs: NavPress, 1994, 2002.

Merton, Thomas. *No Man Is an Island.* Boston: Shambhala Publications, 1955.

Morrison, Erika. *Bandersnatch: An Invitation to Explore Your Unconventional Soul.* Nashville, TN: Thomas Nelson, 2015.

Newell, John Philip. *Listening for the Heartbeat of God: A Celtic Spirituality.* Ramsey, NJ: Paulist Press, 1997.

Purifoy, Christie. *Roots & Sky: A Journey Home in Four Seasons.* Grand Rapids, MI: Revell, 2016.

Rohr, Richard. *The Naked Now.* New York: Crossroad, 2009.

Stafford, Rachel Macy. *Only Love Today: Reminders to Breathe More, Stress Less, and Choose Love*. Grand Rapids, MI: Zondervan, 2017.

Steindl-Rast, Brother David. *Gratefulness, The Heart of Prayer*. Ramsey, NJ: Paulist Press, 1984.

Taylor, Barbara Brown. *An Altar in the World: A Geography of Faith*. New York: HarperOne, 2009.

Woodley, Randy. *Shalom and the Community of Creation: An Indigenous Vision*. Grand Rapids, MI: Wm. B. Eerdmans, 2012.

Ywahoo, Dhyani. *Voices of Our Ancestors: Cherokee Teachings from the Wisdom Fire*. Boston: Shambhala Publications, 1987.

NOTES

Introduction

1   Annie Dillard, *Pilgrim at Tinker Creek* (New York: Harper Perennial, 1974), 11.

Part One

2   J. R. R. Tolkien, *Fellowship of the Ring* (Boston: Houghton Mifflin, 1987), 45.

3   Thomas Merton, *No Man Is an Island* (Boston: Shambhala Publications, 1955), 53.

4   Barbara Brown Taylor, *An Altar in the World: A Geography of Faith* (New York: HarperOne, 2009), 12–13.

5   Ibid.

6   Brother David Steindl-Rast, *Gratefulness, The Heart of Prayer* (Ramsey, NJ: Paulist Press, 1984), 25.

7   Taylor, *An Altar in the World*, 7.

8   Steven Levine, in *For the Love of God: Handbook for the Spirit*, ed. Benjamin Shield and Richard Carlson (Novato, CA: New World Library, 1997), 87.

9   J. R. R. Tolkien, *The Hobbit* (Boston: Ballantine Books, 1966), 290.

10   Henry David Thoreau, *Walden* (Boston: Ticknor and Fields, 1854), 346.

Part Two

11   Glennon Doyle Melton, *Carry On, Warrior: The Power of Embracing Your Messy, Beautiful Life* (New York: Scribner, 2013), 4.

12   David Steindl-Rast, in *For the Love of God*, 92.

13   Albert Einstein, *The World as I See It*, trans. Alan Harris (London: Bodley Head, 1935), 5.

14   Richard Rohr, *The Naked Now* (New York: Crossroad, 2009), 29–30.

15   Jennifer Louden, *Woman's Comfort Book: A Self-Nurturing Guide* (New York: HarperOne, 2005), 2.

16 Edie Wadsworth, in *The Beauty of Grace: Stories of God's Love from Today's Most Popular Writers*, ed. Dawn Camp (Grand Rapids, MI: Revell, 2015), 87.

17 Louisa May Alcott, *Little Men: Life at Plumfield with Jo's Boys* (Boston: Roberts Brothers, 1871), 31.

18 Richard Foster, *Prayer: Finding the Heart's True Home* (New York: HarperOne, 2002), 15.

19 Wendell Berry, *Standing by Words: Essays* (Berkeley, CA: Counterpoint, 1983), 14.

Part Three

20 Rachel Held Evans, *Searching for Sunday* (Nashville, TN: Belson Books, 2015), 204–5.

21 Walt Whitman, from the poem "A Song for Occupations" in *Leaves of Grass* (Boston: Thayer and Eldridge, 1860–61), 157.

22 Frederick Buechner, *Beyond Words: Daily Readings in the ABC's of Faith* (New York: HarperOne, 2004), 139.

23 Anne Lamott, *Help, Thanks, Wow* (New York: Riverhead Books, 2012), 7.

24 Richard Rohr, *Falling Upward: A Spirituality for the Two Halves of Life* (San Francisco: Jossey-Bass, 2011), 159.

25 Geraldine Brooks, *Caleb's Crossing* (New York: Penguin Books, 2012), 292.

Part Four

26 Helen Keller, *Let Us Have Faith* (Garden City, NY: Doubleday, Doran, 1940), 51.

27 "The Gorsedd Prayer," as rendered in *Yours Is the Day, Lord, Yours Is the Night*, ed. Jeanie and David Gushee (Nashville, TN: Thomas Nelson, 2012), 248.

28 Richard Foster, *Celebration of Discipline, 20th Anniversary Edition* (San Francisco: HarperSanFrancisco, 2002), 97.

29 Taylor, *An Altar in the World*, 91.

30 Frederick Buechner, *Wishful Thinking: A Seeker's ABC* (San Francisco: HarperSanFrancisco, 1973), 119.

31 Emily Dickinson, excerpt from letter in Thomas Wentworth Higginson, "Emily Dickinson's Letters," *The Atlantic*, October 1891, accessed September 30, 2016, http://www.theatlantic.com/past/unbound/poetry/emilyd/edletter.htm.

32 Dhyani Ywahoo, *Voices of Our Ancestors: Cherokee Teachings from the Wisdom Fire* (Boston, MA: Shambhala Publications, 1987), 59.

33 Stanley Hauerwas, "The Sanctified Body: Why Perfection Does Not Require a 'Self,'" in *Sanctify Them in Truth: Holiness Exemplified* (Nashville, TN: Abingdon Press, 1998), 79.

34 Richard Rohr, *The Naked Now*, 102

35 Amber Haines, *Wild in the Hollow* (Grand Rapids, MI: Revell, 2015), 32

Part Five

36 C. S. Lewis, *The Lion, the Witch and the Wardrobe* (New York: HarperCollins, 2008), 79.

37 Fyodor Dostoevsky, *The Brothers Karamazov*, trans. Richard Pevear and Larissa Volokhonsky (New York: Farrar, Straus and Giroux, 1990), 776.

38 Victor Hugo, *William Shakespeare* (Chicago: A.C. McClurg 1887), 91.

Part Six

39 Randy Woodley, *Shalom and the Community of Creation: An Indigenous Vision* (Grand Rapids, MI: Wm. B. Eerdmans, 2012), 20.

40 J. Philip Newell, *Listening for the Heartbeat of God: A Celtic Spirituality* (Ramsey, NJ: Paulist Press, 1997), 70.

41 Deepak Chopra, *Why Is God Laughing? The Path to Joy & Spiritual Optimism* (New York: Three Rivers Press, 2008), 129.

42 Rohr, *The Naked Now*, 77.

43 Antonio Porchia, *Voices*, trans. W. S. Merwin (Port Townsend, WA: Copper Canyon Press, 2003), 11.

44 "Cherokee Words of Wisdom," Cherokees of California Inc., accessed September 30, 2016, http://www.powersource.com/cocinc/articles/wisdom.htm.

Part Seven

45 Howard Murphet, in *For the Love of God*, 38.

46 Newell, *Listening for the Heartbeat of God*, 99.

47 Erika Morrison, *Bandersnatch: An Invitation to Explore Your Unconventional Soul* (Nashville, TN: Thomas Nelson], 2015), 219.

48   Thoreau, *Walden*, 339.

49   Leif Enger, *Peace Like a River* (New York: Grove Press, 2001), 311.

50   Christie Purifoy, *Roots & Sky: A Journey Home in Four Seasons* (Grand Rapids, MI: Revell, 2016), 37.

Part Eight

51   Tenzin Gyatso, in *For the Love of God*, 4.

52   Rachel Macy Stafford, *Hands Free Life: Nine Habits for Overcoming Distraction, Living Better, and Loving More* (Grand Rapids, MI: Zondervan, 2015), 66.

53   Jan Karon, *Out to Canaan* (New York: Viking, 1997), 49–50.

54   Lola Ridge, "Wind in the Alleys," *The Atlantic*, May 12, 1920.

55   Dillard, *Pilgrim at Tinker Creek*, 79.

56   J. K. Rowling, *Harry Potter and the Sorcerer's Stone* (New York: Scholastic, 1993), 306.

ABOUT PARACLETE PRESS

Who We Are

Paraclete Press is a publisher of books, recordings, and DVDs on Christian spirituality. Our publishing represents a full expression of Christian belief and practice—from Catholic to Evangelical, from Protestant to Orthodox.

We are the publishing arm of the Community of Jesus, an ecumenical monastic community in the Benedictine tradition. As such, we are uniquely positioned in the marketplace without connection to a large corporation and with informal relationships to many branches and denominations of faith.

What We Are Doing

PARACLETE PRESS BOOKS | Paraclete publishes books that show the richness and depth of what it means to be Christian. Although Benedictine spirituality is at the heart of who we are and all that we do, we publish books that reflect the Christian experience across many cultures, time periods, and houses of worship. We publish books that nourish the vibrant life of the church and its people.

We have several different series, including the bestselling Paraclete Essentials and Paraclete Giants series of classic texts in contemporary English; Voices from the Monastery—men and women monastics writing about living a spiritual life today; our award-winning Paraclete Poetry series as well as the Mount Tabor Books on the arts; bestselling gift books for children on the occasions of baptism and first communion; and the Active Prayer Series that brings creativity and liveliness to any life of prayer.

MOUNT TABOR BOOKS | Paraclete's newest series, Mount Tabor Books, focuses on the arts and literature as well as liturgical worship and spirituality, and was created in conjunction with the Mount Tabor Ecumenical Centre for Art and Spirituality in Barga, Italy.

PARACLETE RECORDINGS | From Gregorian chant to contemporary American choral works, our recordings celebrate the best of sacred choral music composed through the centuries that create a space for heaven and earth to intersect. Paraclete Recordings is the record label representing the internationally acclaimed choir Gloriæ Dei Cantores, praised for their "rapt and fathomless spiritual intensity" by *American Record Guide*; the Gloriæ Dei Cantores Schola, specializing in the study and performance of Gregorian chant; and the other instrumental artists of the Arts Empowering Life Foundation.

Paraclete Press is also privileged to be the exclusive North American distributor of the recordings of the Monastic Choir of St. Peter's Abbey in Solesmes, France, long considered to be a leading authority on Gregorian chant.

PARACLETE VIDEO | Our DVDs offer spiritual help, healing, and biblical guidance for a broad range of life issues including grief and loss, marriage, forgiveness, facing death, bullying, addictions, Alzheimer's, and spiritual formation.

Learn more about us at our website:
www.paracletepress.com or phone us toll-free at 1.800.451.5006

SCAN
TO
READ
MORE

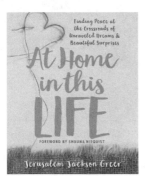